T0230906

CompuServe 2000
Made Simple

Keith Brindley

Routledge
Taylor & Francis Group

LONDON AND NEW YORK

First published 2000 by Made Simple

2 Park Square, Milton Park, Abingdon, Oxon OX14 4RN
711 Third Avenue, New York, NY 10017, USA

Routledge is an imprint of the Taylor and Francis Group, an informa business

First issued in hardback 2017

Copyright © Keith Brindley 2000

All rights reserved. No part of this book may be reprinted or reproduced or
utilised in any form or by any electronic, mechanical, or other means, now
known or hereafter invented, including photocopying and recording, or in
any information storage or retrieval system, without permission in writing
from the publishers.

Notice:
Product or corporate names may be trademarks or registered trademarks, and
are used only for identification and explanation without intent to infringe.

TRADEMARKS/REGISTERED TRADEMARKS
Computer hardware and software brand names mentioned in this
book are protected by their respective trademarks and are acknowledged

British Library Cataloguing in Publication Data

A catalogue record for this book is available from the British Library

ISBN 978-0-7506-4524-9 (pbk)
ISBN 978-1-138-43620-6 (hbk)
ISBN 978-0-7506-4525-6 — CompuServe edition

Typeset and produced by Co-publications, Loughborough
Set in Archetype, Cotswold, Bash and Gravity from Advanced Graphics Limited
All screenshots taken with Screen Thief for Windows from Nildram Software (info@nildram.co.uk)
Icons designed by Sarah Ward © 1994

FOR EVERY TITLE THAT WE PUBLISH, BUTTERWORTH-HEINEMANN
WILL PAY FOR BTCV TO PLANT AND CARE FOR A TREE.

Contents

Foreword

Welcome to CompuServe!

CompuServe 2000 is our latest software and we're proud to endorse this book as the official guide to what we believe is an outstanding Internet service.

CompuServe 2000 was developed to fulfil the needs of a new breed of Internet user, people with busy lives and increasing demands on their time. With this in mind, we've built a new navigation and menu system to make it easier and quicker to get around online. Communication tools like e-mail and Instant Messenger will make your electronic communication fast, effective and fun. CompuServe 2000 also gives you access to a huge range of information, all organised to ensure you're never more than a few clicks away from what you need, whether it's an analysis of your favourite team's performance, a vital business report, information on mortgages and savings, or the latest theory on health and fitness. There are also special time-saving tools to help you manage your shares, research and book travel arrangements, access the service when you travel abroad — in fact, something for every area of your life.

This book also marks an important milestone for the company as we enter a new phase of growth.

CompuServe was the founding father of the Internet. When we began more than 30 years ago, we offered one of the only reliable ways to transport large data files around the world and we provided data processing for businesses when computers were not affordable.

From this grew the Internet, a technology that has surpassed everyone's expectations. So far, it's been adopted at a faster rate than television, and Internet access has become commonplace both at work and at home. With such a bewildering choice of Internet service providers, CompuServe's reputation for quality and reliability is serving us well; we're now part of Europe's leading Internet and e-commerce services company.

The CompuServe service has evolved constantly since that time but our broader objective hasn't changed. We're more dedicated to our customers than ever and evangelical in our mission to help them achieve their aspirations.

No-one can say where the boundaries for this technology lie, but one thing is certain — you're joining one of the most interesting and exciting Internet communities in the world.

Enjoy your time online.

David Fischer
General Manager, CompuServe UK

Preface

In terms of users, CompuServe is one of the largest online services, as well as being the most established. Indeed, CompuServe has millions of users worldwide, who all regularly dial-in to the CompuServe system over a network of telephone lines, modems, ISDN links, the Internet and other related communications methods, for a low-cost service which comprises e-mail, file transfer, World Wide Web browsing, chatting with other members, communications with members of special interest groups and so on.

What I'm getting at, is that CompuServe is a big system. And I mean B–I–G! The services it offers are wide-ranging, tremendous, remarkable, and incredibly useful. However, because of this, new (and even existing) users can sometimes be over-awed by their extent. That's where this book can help.

Finally, I have to say that CompuServe — while being incredibly big — is a dynamic service. That's a posh way to say that the information content available changes to suit new and existing users' requirements, and is being added to at a rate of knots! In real terms for you and me, all this means is that some of the services and features might have changed a little between me writing about them and you reading about them. Their use, however, remains little altered — only how you might access them might be different.

CompuServe 2000 is a wonderful system. It has something for everyone. I hope you enjoy it, and I hope you enjoy this book.

Keith Brindley

1 CompuServe

What is CompuServe?

CompuServe is an Internet online service...

...so now you know.

To understand what it does, though, requires a little history. A long time ago, the only computers available were very large and very expensive mainframe ones. Often the only form of computing feasible to people was to access a mainframe computer connected with a standard telephone line to a remote terminal. Very often, larger companies who had a mainframe computer would rent out use of the mainframe this way.

One US company, Golden United Life Insurance, did just that. In 1969 the company adopted the CompuServe name.

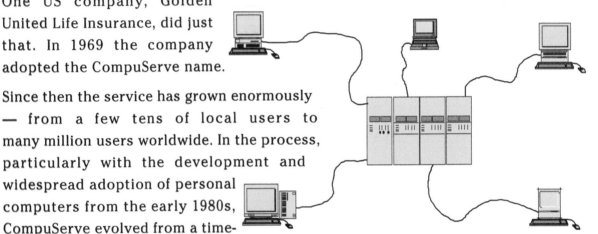

Since then the service has grown enormously — from a few tens of local users to many million users worldwide. In the process, particularly with the development and widespread adoption of personal computers from the early 1980s, CompuServe evolved from a time-sharing computer space rental system to — first — an online service, then — second — and very much more important; to an Internet online service.

OK, so what's an online service?

Although the meaning is not particularly well defined, an online service is usually thought to be a computer system which other computers can login to — usually over a telephone line — to access data and communicate with other users of the service — usually worldwide. The data is not just raw computer data, however (as it would be in the mainframe/ terminal method that CompuServe initially was back in 1969). Instead it's organised into hierarchies, folders and files, so users can locate rapidly the things they want in a user-friendly way. However, despite being accessible worldwide, online services are closed systems — in that members can't get out, and outsiders can't get in.

And what's this Internet thing then?

In its basic structure, the Internet is a vast collection of connected computer networks. Any computer can get connected to the Internet if it follows Internet standards — see page 60. Usually, these networks are run by organisations which allow users to access the Internet.

After this, however, the Internet — and all the computer data contained therein, as well as the uses to which users themselves put it to — is limitless, and **very** fluid. It can be very daunting locating data you want on the Internet if you're not sure what you're looking for (unlike online services, with their pyramid-like arrangement — see page 9). Also, new Internet services appear regularly, sometimes going out of fashion as rapidly as they appear, sometimes becoming extremely popular. Indeed, one of the most popular parts of the Internet today is the World Wide Web (see page 60) which saw its first light of day only eight years ago, yet which effectively opens the world out to anyone with a computer and modem.

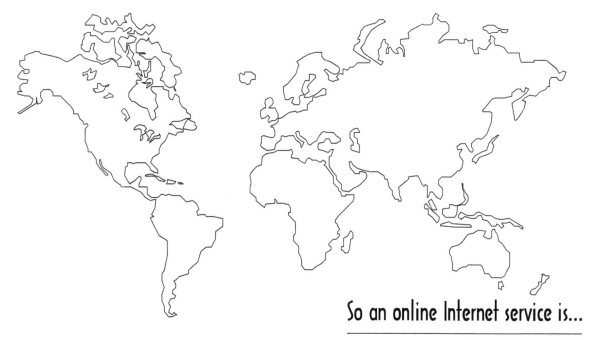

So an online Internet service is...

Yes, that's right. On the one hand, CompuServe is an Internet service provider that effectively rents Internet access out to its members, allowing full Internet access with all its facets. On the other hand, CompuServe has lost none of its user-friendliness as it still retains its comfortable closed online service alongside the open Internet access you get with it. In other words, CompuServe is the best of both worlds!

3

Launching CompuServe 2000

Basic steps:

The CompuServe program you launch to gain access to the CompuServe service is known as a CompuServe client. The current version of the CompuServe client is called CompuServe 2000, to differentiate it from earlier versions.

The first thing you ever do when using CompuServe 2000 is to start up the program. There are several methods.

STARTUP FROM THE DESKTOP

1 Locate the CompuServe 2000 icon on your desktop. It's usually found in the **CompuServe 2000** folder on your computer's hard drive. Double-click the icon to start CompuServe 2000

OR:

2 Locate the **CompuServe 2000** shortcut icon on the main desktop and double-click it to start CompuServe 2000

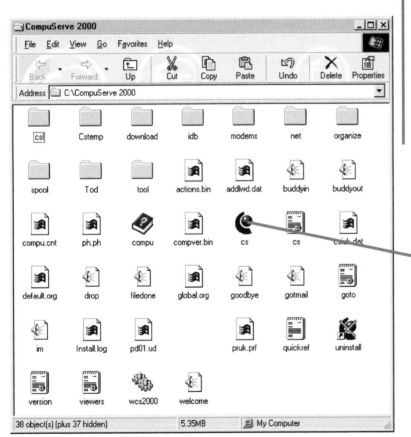

1 Locate the CompuServe 2000 icon and double-click it

There may be a shortcut on the desktop — double-click it to start CompuServe 2000

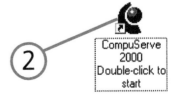

2 CompuServe 2000 Double-click to start

4

3 You can also locate the CompuServe 2000 program in the **Start** menu. It should be in the **CompuServe 2000** folder, within the **Programs** folder of the **Start** menu

OR:

4 If your computer has not been altered since CompuServe was first installed, you should also notice a shortcut directly in the first level of the **Start** menu. As a result, you can startup CompuServe simply by choosing **Start↳ CompuServe 2000**

OR:

5 A CompuServe icon should also be in the Quick Launch toolbar. Click the icon to start CompuServe 2000

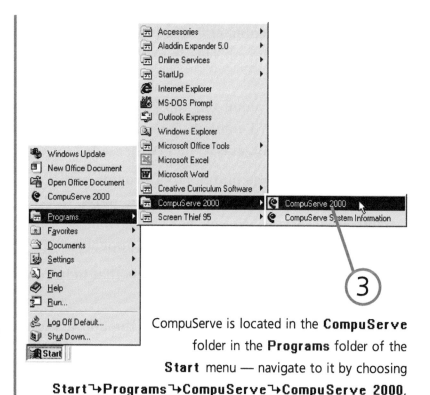

CompuServe is located in the **CompuServe** folder in the **Programs** folder of the **Start** menu — navigate to it by choosing **Start↳Programs↳CompuServe↳CompuServe 2000**, then release the mouse to startup CompuServe 2000

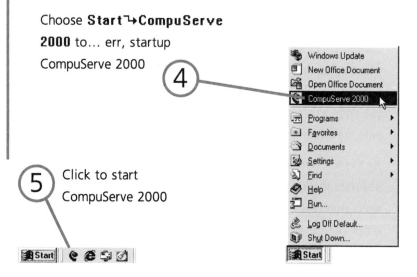

Choose **Start↳CompuServe 2000** to... err, startup CompuServe 2000

Click to start CompuServe 2000

CompuServe 2000

When you launch CompuServe 2000 the main application window is displayed. This is organised into four main parts:

1 top menu bar — along the top of the application window. The standard computing menus — File, Edit, Access, Window, Help, and so on are displayed here

2 toolbar — with large buttons that provide one-click menu-style or instant access to main parts of the CompuServe service. As you click a button, a drop-down menu, further option, or service appears

3 navigation buttons — smaller buttons that help you access particular features

4 main page area — the remainder of the application window displays whatever service or feature you access within CompuServe.

Take note:

The display shown here is the basic display for the whole of the CompuServe 2000 service. While the display changes a little as you make your way around the CompuServe system and beyond onto the Internet, it's actually very similar — wherever you are.

As a result, once you've got the hang of this basic display, you'll understand what to do wherever you find yourself to be. And — more important — the basic display here is the control centre from which you can get around the whole system

① The top menu bar — a conventional menu bar from which you can choose selections from drop-down menus

② Top buttons along the toolbar — clicking a button produces either a drop-down menu or instant access to shortcuts for commonly-used services — see pages 28–29

③ Navigation buttons — allowing you to step backwards and forwards through pages you access — see page 29

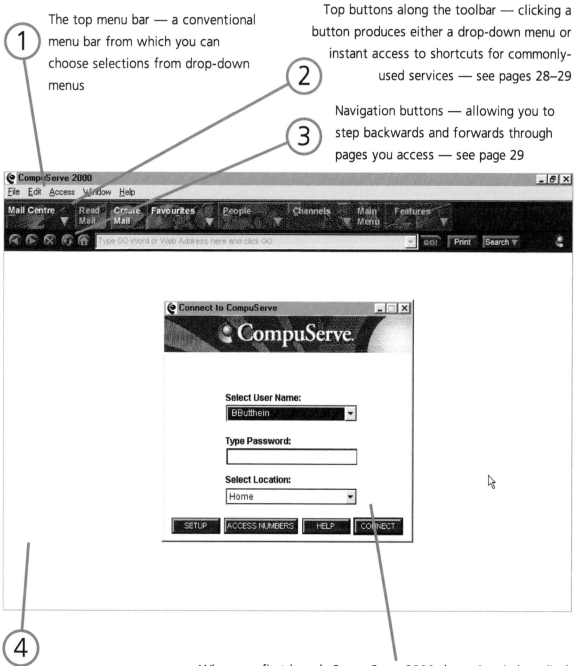

④ The main page area — whatever service you access within CompuServe is displayed here

When you first launch CompuServe 2000 the main window displays the **Connect to CompuServe** dialog box. From here you can connect to CompuServe, change the CompuServe client setup, or get help. All these topics are covered in detail later, on pages 10–11

Where in the world

Once you ve launched CompuServe 2000 and you re in CompuServe, there s a whole world of information: information about entertainment, about finance, about news, about media, about education, about the Internet, about travel, about sport, about information, about

well, yes, about everything, really. It s all there!

CompuServe 2000 is your starting point to finding and using all this information and, as such, you should have some idea of what you can access directly from it.

CompuServe 2000 is simply a tool you use to access the CompuServe network s hierarchical layers. Imagine a pyramid, with the main menu as the pyramid s apex. From there, you can locate most things with just two or three clicks of buttons or page tabs.

The diagram showing the main menu this way should, hopefully, give you some idea of where things are located within the CompuServe network. Look lower down in the pyramid, to find the service you want, then retrace its route up the Main Menu pyramid. Finally, just chose relevant Main Menu selections, or click buttons or links to get to the service.

Take note:

A warning Ñ before you start clicking buttons and page tabs, you should be aware that doing so could result in CompuServe 2000 attempting to log you onto the CompuServe service.

Checkout the next four pages to see what happens as you log on and Ñ more important Ñ find out how to log off too, before you spend a fortune in phone calls!

Tip:

Once youÕe online to the CompuServe network and you have accessed one of CompuServeÕ services, the display might change somewhat. To get back to base, from wherever you are when using CompuServe 2000, click the Main Menu top button on CompuServe 2000

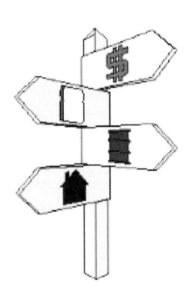

Click the Main Menu button to
get back here — at any time

Click menu buttons to
reach menus

Main Menu

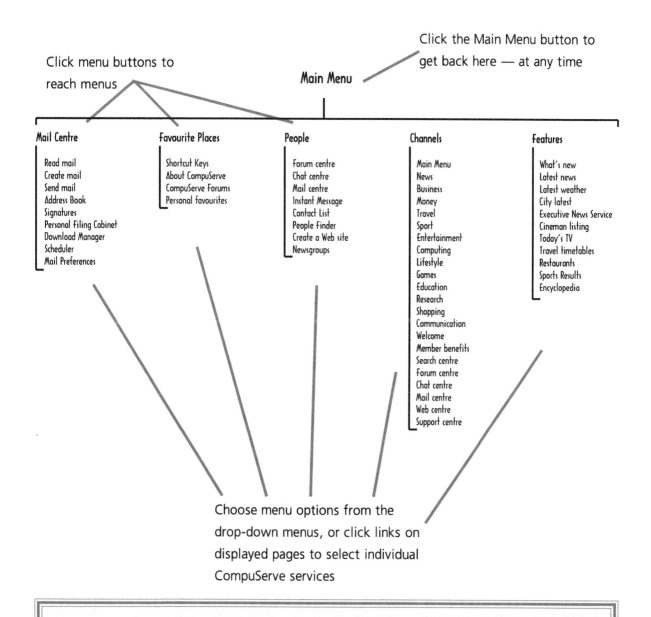

Mail Centre	Favourite Places	People	Channels	Features
Read mail	Shortcut Keys	Forum centre	Main Menu	What's new
Create mail	About CompuServe	Chat centre	News	Latest news
Send mail	CompuServe Forums	Mail centre	Business	Latest weather
Address Book	Personal favourites	Instant Message	Money	City latest
Signatures		Contact List	Travel	Executive News Service
Personal Filing Cabinet		People Finder	Sport	Cineman listing
Download Manager		Create a Web site	Entertainment	Today's TV
Scheduler		Newsgroups	Computing	Travel timetables
Mail Preferences			Lifestyle	Restaurants
			Games	Sports Results
			Education	Encyclopedia
			Research	
			Shopping	
			Communication	
			Welcome	
			Member benefits	
			Search centre	
			Forum centre	
			Chat centre	
			Mail centre	
			Web centre	
			Support centre	

Choose menu options from the
drop-down menus, or click links on
displayed pages to select individual
CompuServe services

Tip:

While this diagram refers only to the Main Menu — that's enough to be getting along with, isn't it? — the other displays you'll come across within CompuServe 2000 are similar — and, in fact, are all based around it. If you need further information about any particular display, however, CompuServe 2000's built-in help system is always there to help you. Read pages 20—25 for further details

Connecting to CompuServe

Basic steps:

If your computer is setup correctly and just as CompuServe 2000 was installed, the CompuServe network is available to you from CompuServe 2000 with just the click of a button.

 Choose **Access↪Connect Screen** if the **Connect to CompuServe** dialog box is not displayed

1 If the **Connect to CompuServe** dialog box is not displayed, choose **Access↪Connect Screen**, or type `Ctrl`+`K` to call it up

2 Enter your password

③ Click **CONNECT**

3 Click the **CONNECT** button to connect to CompuServe

② Type your password

Logging on

In connecting, there's a log on process which CompuServe 2000 goes through to get you online. The **Connection** dialog box leads you visually through all this — you don't need to take another step if you're happy with the connection going on.

If you're not happy, on the other hand (say, you clicked a button by mistake, and don't want to log on at this time) simply click the **Cancel** button to stop the log on process.

Tip:

You can have upto seven different User Names on your CompuServe account. Pages 130–131 show you how to setup other User Names

Basic steps:

1 Click the drop-down menu arrow of the **Select User Name** field to access the special **Guest** User Name

2 Click the **Select Location** field drop-down menu arrow, to choose the method you want to use to connect to CompuServe

3 Click the **SETUP** button to change CompuServe 2000's connect methods

4 Click the **HELP** button to access CompuServe 2000's help system

Take note:

When you first start to use CompuServe 2000, the only location you'll find at step 2 will be the initial one – probably labelled Home. You only need to add other locations if you want to connect to CompuServe from other places

The **Connect to CompuServe** dialog box has other uses too. If you want, you can allow other CompuServe users to connect to CompuServe as guests (alternatively, you can connect on someone else's computer this way).

The **Connect to CompuServe** dialog box can be also used to setup your CompuServe 2000 program to connect to CompuServe from other locations (say, you are abroad and want to check your e-mail from your laptop computer) or in another way (say, with another modem, or over a local area network — see pages 148–149).

Finally, it's also a valuable way to access CompuServe 2000's built-in help system.

Minimize the **Connect to** dialog box by clicking here

Close the **Connect to** dialog box by clicking here

Click the drop-down menu arrow, and choose from entries here

Click the drop-down menu here, and choose from locations here

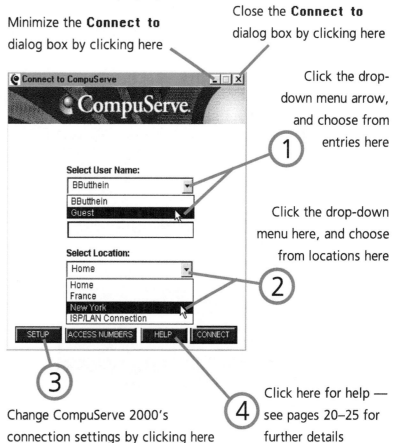

Change CompuServe 2000's connection settings by clicking here

Click here for help — see pages 20–25 for further details

Logging off CompuServe

When you're logged onto CompuServe, there are some visual indications that you're online.

To log off from CompuServe, there are three main methods: shown here.

The easiest way to see if you're online is to watch the toolbar — these buttons are active when online, and inactive (greyed out) when offline. Also, if you have mail to read, the **Read Mail** button is in yellow print

Basic steps:

1 Choose **Access↳ Disconnect** or type `Ctrl`+`D`

OR:

2 Choose **File↳Exit**, or type `Alt`+`F4`

OR:

3 Click the **Close** button

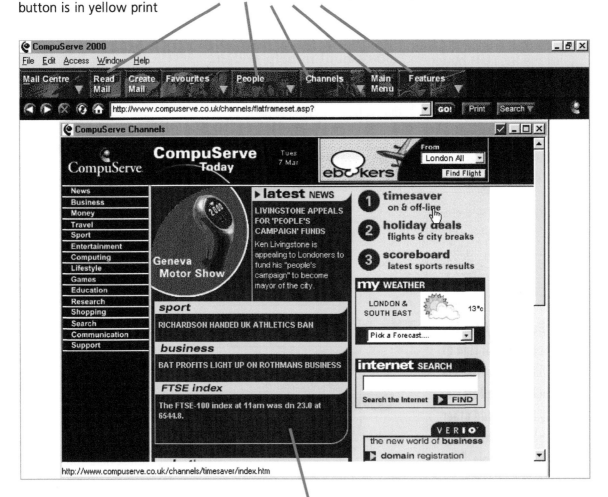

A page in the page area of the main window shows you're online

GO...

If you know the CompuServe service you want, the **GO** command is one of the best access methods.

Most CompuServe services are given a quick-reference word (known as a **GO** word). If you know what the **GO** word for a particular service is, you can get there as quickly as typing the **GO** word into a **GO Word** dialog box and pressing the **GO** button. See the next page to find out what the GO words are.

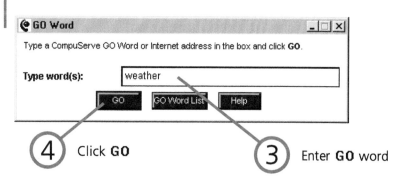

Tip:

You don't need to call up a GO Word dialog box to use GO words. Just type the GO word into the text box on the navigation toolbar, then click the GO! button immediately to its right

GO... to the Internet, too

One of the beauties of the **GO** word system, is that you can even access the Internet from a **GO Word** dialog box. Instead of a pure CompuServe **GO** word, just enter the Internet URL address and CompuServe 2000 takes you there. See page 62 for a description of Internet URLs.

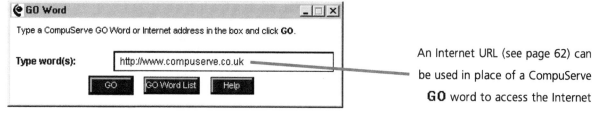

An Internet URL (see page 62) can be used in place of a CompuServe **GO** word to access the Internet

GO (contd)

GO is a great way to get around CompuServe. However, that's only if you know the GO word for the service you want. In the GO Word dialog box, you'll have noticed the GO Word List button. This is the key to finding out about GO words.

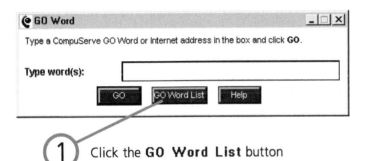

① Click the GO Word List button

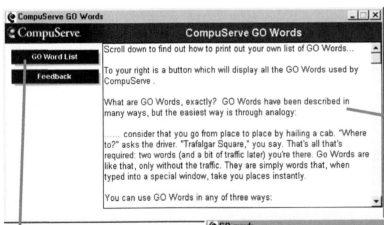

③ Click GO Word List

Click the button you want

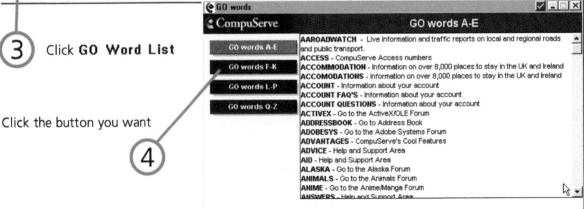

④

Read the GO
information

1. With the GO Word dialog box visible, click the GO Word List button

2. The resultant Compu-Serve GO Words dialog box gives information about GO words — read it if you are unfamiliar with GO words and their use

3. Click the GO Word List button

4. Click the alphabetical group button you expect the GO word to be in

5 In the resultant **GO Word List**, scroll down to locate the service you want, then double-click it to choose it

6 Choose **Edit⁀Copy**, or type `Ctrl`+`C` to copy the word

7 Close the word list

8 Choose **Edit⁀Paste**, or type `Ctrl`+`V` to paste the word in the **GO Word** dialog box

9 Click the **GO** button to access the service

Going back...

A list of services you've visited recently appears in the drop-down box in the toolbar. This provides you with an extremely handy method of re-accessing services (and Internet URLs you've recently visited).

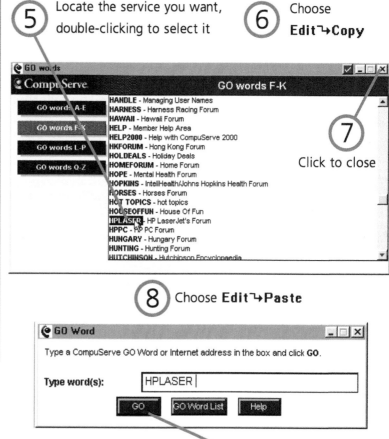

(5) Locate the service you want, double-clicking to select it

(6) Choose **Edit⁀Copy**

(7) Click to close

(8) Choose **Edit⁀Paste**

(9) Click **GO** to access the service

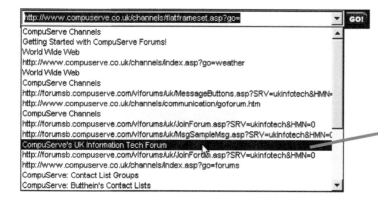

Scroll down the list to locate the service you want, clicking it to select it

Favourite Places

CompuServe 2000 allows you to keep your own list of services and other places (such as Internet URLs) you visit regularly. It's called **Favourite Places**. Some important places are already installed for you, and you can easily add your own, or edit or delete the existing services.

There are three things you need to know about using Favourite Places:

▷ accessing the Favourite Places themselves

▷ setting up Favourite Places so they are easily and neatly accessible

▷ adding your own Favourite Places.

USING FAVOURITE PLACES:

1 Click the **Favourites** button on the toolbar

2 Point the mouse cursor over the lower items in the drop-down menu (hierarchical items will open out to show sub-menu items)

3 Click the Favourite Place you want

Using Favourite Places

Favourite Places are accessed as a simple menu choice.

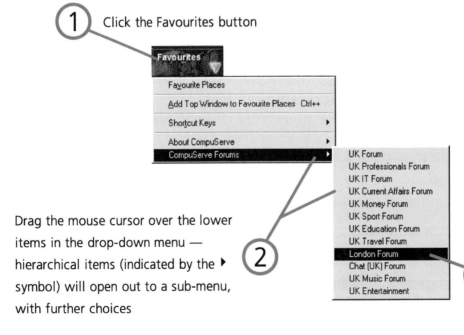

1 Click the Favourites button

Drag the mouse cursor over the lower items in the drop-down menu — hierarchical items (indicated by the ▶ symbol) will open out to a sub-menu, with further choices

2

3 When you have located the Favourite Place you want, click it

Setting up Favourite Places

SETTING UP YOUR FAVOURITES:

1   Choose **Favourites↪ Favourite Places**

2   Open out any folders within the Favourite Places window, by double-clicking the folder

3   If you know a service's **GO** word, or Internet place's URL, you can create a Favourite Place directly, by clicking the **New** button

4   In the **Add New Folder/Favourite Place** dialog box, enter a description

5   Enter the Internet URL (see page 62), or **GO** word

6   Click **OK**

contd...

While — as you'll see soon — it's easy to add Favourite Places, it's usually necessary to take charge of them, in order to keep them neat, tidy, and as easy to access as possible.

Favourite Places are stored in the Favourite Places window, either loose, or in folders.

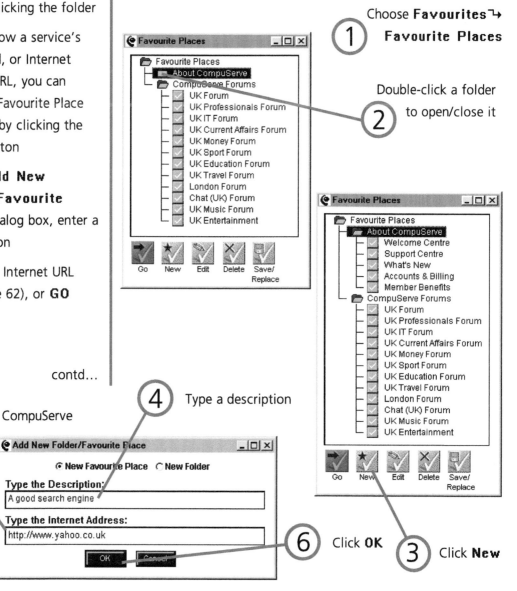

Choose **Favourites↪ Favourite Places** ①

Double-click a folder ② to open/close it

Type a description ④

Type a URL or CompuServe **GO** word

⑤

Click **OK** ⑥

③ Click **New**

Favourite Places (contd)

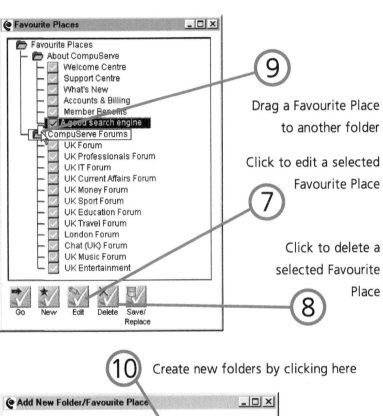

Drag a Favourite Place
to another folder

Click to edit a selected
Favourite Place

Click to delete a
selected Favourite
Place

Create new folders by clicking here

7 If you want to change a
Favourite Place, click the
Edit button — you can
edit both the description
and the Internet URL

8 Click the **Delete** button
to delete the selected
Favourite Place

9 Drag a Favourite Place
within the **Favourite
Places** window to move
it to a new position and
keep the window tidy

10 Create a new folder,
rather than a new Favour-
ite Place, by clicking the
New Folder radio
button of the **Add New
Folder/Favourite
Place** dialog box

Tip:

Folders can be nested
within other folders in the
Favourite Places
window — to further organ-
ise your Favourite Places
hierarchically

Take note:

Note that in the example of creating a new Favourite Place, in
steps 3–6, the new Favourite Place is created in the folder
previously highlighted in the Favourite Places window – in
other words, to position a new Favourite Place in any particular
folder, highlight the folder you want to store the new Favourite
Place in, prior to creating it

ADDING YOUR FAVOURITES:

1 Wherever you are within CompuServe, store it as a Favourite Place by clicking the Favourite Place button ✅

2 In the **Insert a Favourite Place** dialog box click the **Insert in Favourites** button

OR:

3 Drag and drop the Favourite Place button ✅ to the Favourites menu

Adding your own Favourite Places

CompuServe 2000 makes the process of adding your own Favourite Places a snap — you can even direct the Favourite Place to a friend.

Click to store in your **Favourite Places** window ②

Click to forward to someone else

Drag and drop the button to the Favourites menu ③

Click the Favourite Place button ①

Help me – I'm drowning!

CompuServe 2000 has a powerful help facility built-in. This can be extremely useful if, for example, you can't remember what a tool does, or if you find yourself lost in the vastness of the Internet.

CompuServe 2000's in-built help comes in two forms:

▷ first are tool tips — little labels which show up when you point over any of the buttons on a toolbar

▷ second is the general Help feature — you can access this at any time, for help about any feature, service, command or topic. There's a number of ways you can use the feature to obtain the help you need at any particular point.

TOOL TIPS

1 Position your pointer over any button on a toolbar to see the button's name as a label

HELP — MAIN WINDOW

2 Choose **Help↪Search for Help on**..., or click the **Help** button in any window that has one

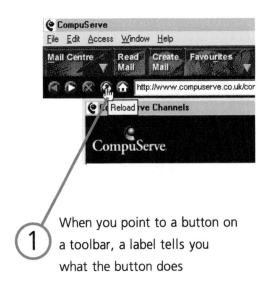

① When you point to a button on a toolbar, a label tells you what the button does

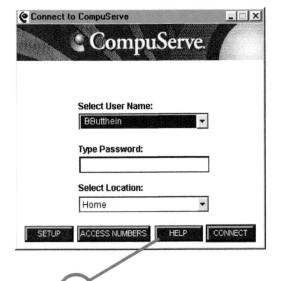

② Help is available from any window that has a **Help** button, or by choosing **Help↪Search for Help on**...

Basic steps:

1 After calling up the **Help** window (step 2, left), click the **Contents** tab

2 Help is shown as either individual topics (with a page icon), or as grouped topics (with a book icon)

3 Select a book icon

4 Click the **Open** button (or simply double-click the icon at step 3) to open the group and display its topics

5 Similarly, select then click the **Open** button for, or double-click, nested book icons to display their topics

6 When you locate the topic you want help with, select it, then click the **Display** button (or simply double-click its page icon)

7 Read the topic

Open nested grouped topics ⑤

Open a topic ⑥

Help by Contents

Of the ways you can get help from within CompuServe 2000, Help by Contents is the first we look at.

Help Topics: CompuServe 2000 Help ? ✕

Contents | Index | Find

Click a book, and then click Open. Or click another tab, such as Index.

📖 Getting Assistance
　? About The Member Centre
　? Getting billing information
　? Getting help online
　? Telephone Support ——— Individual topic
　📚 Connecting to CompuServe
　📚 Communicating with Others
　📚 Using E-mail ——— Grouped topic
　📚 Using CompuServe Features
　📚 Keeping Your Account Secure
　📚 Managing Your Account and User Names
　📚 Navigating Online
　📚 Troubleshooting

③ Select a grouped topic icon

[Open] [Print...] [Cancel]

① Click the **Contents** tab

②

④ Click **Open**

Help Topics: CompuServe 2000 Help

Contents | Index | Find

Click a topic, and then click Display. Or click anothe

　? Getting help online
　? Telephone Support
　📚 Connecting to CompuServe
　📚 Communicating with Others
　📖 Using E-mail
　　📖 E-mail Basics
　　　? What's my e-mail address?
　　　? Sending e-mail
　　　? Determining if your e-mail has been r
　　　? How do I know I have e-mail?
　　　? Reading e-mail
　　　? Reading your saved e-mail
　　　? Sending e-mail to Internet addresses
　　　? Using automatic quoting in e-mail responses
　　　? Recovering a deleted e-mail message

[Display] [Print...] [Cancel]

CompuServe 2000 Help ＿▢✕
File Edit Bookmark Options Help
[Help Topics] [Back] [Print] [<<]
[>>]

📄 **To read e-mail in your online mailbox**

1 Connect to the CompuServe service.
2 Click the **Read Mail** icon on the toolbar. (If your toolbar is compacted, the icon label says **Read**.)
3 Double-click an e-mail message to read it.

Notes

• You can set a mail preference to keep e-mail in your online mailbox for up to 7 days after it has been opened.

• The more you use e-mail, the more you may want to use CompuServe Scheduler to manage your e-mail.

❓ How do I know I have e-mail?
　Related Topics

⑦ Read the topic

Related topics may be shown — click them to access

I'm still drowning...

Help by Index

There are other ways to access the Help system too. You can — with Help by Index — type in the word or phrase you are looking for help on.

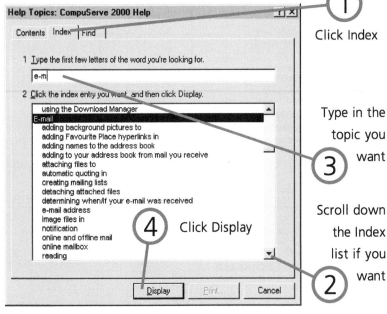

Click Index

Type in the topic you want

Scroll down the Index list if you want

Click Display

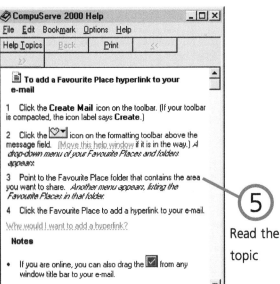

Read the topic

Basic steps:

1 After calling up the **Help** window (step 2, page 20), click the **Index** tab

2 Help is shown as a list of topics — you can scroll down the list to locate the topic you want help with

3 Best, though, is to start to type in the word or phrase you are looking for — the Help feature will jump to the grouped topic in the list corresponding to it

4 When you locate the topic in the group that you want, click the **Display** button (or simply double-click the topic)

5 Read the topic contents

Tip:

For the first 30 days you use CompuServe 2000, everytime you log on you'll see Ernie the Owl. If you click his window's Click Here button, you'll reach the Getting Started guide to using CompuServe 2000

Basic steps:

1 After calling up the **Help** window (step 2, page 20), click the **Find** tab

2 Begin to type a word you are looking for— the Help feature will jump to phrases it finds beginning with the letters you type

3 Select the word you want

4 Click the **Display** button

5 The **Help** window lists topics containing the word — click one

Tip:

If all else fails, you can mail (see pages xx–xx) or telephone CompuServe for help directly:

▷ **mail** ukcssvc – **for general or billing help**

▷ **mail** ukcstech – **for technical queries**

▷ **phone 0870 6000 800 – 8am to midnight daily (except Christmas Day)**

Help by Find

The final way to use CompuServe 2000's in-built help system, is by making it find the topic you want — in a simple yet powerful wordsearch technique.

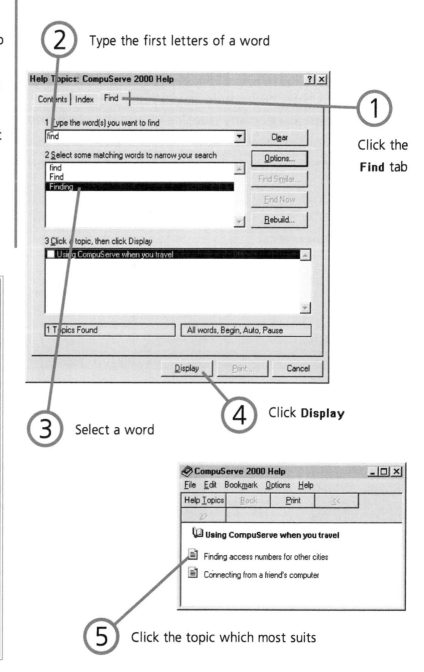

② Type the first letters of a word

① Click the **Find** tab

③ Select a word

④ Click **Display**

⑤ Click the topic which most suits

23

...gurgle, still drowning!

Online help

While CompuServe 2000's in-built help system is very useful, occasionally it still can't answer the questions you might have about CompuServe 2000 or the CompuServe network.

In such instances, further help is available online — the beauty about this online help is that (as it is online) it can reflect and answer any queries about the changing face of CompuServe. Any new features added to the network, for example, can be described and supported instantly.

Much of CompuServe's online help is accessed through the Member Services.

Basic steps:

1 Connect to the CompuServe network

2 Choose **Help↳ Support Centre**

3 In the **Member Services** dialog box, click either the button on the left corresponding to the area you want help on, or its title in the descriptive section on the right — in this example the **Manage Your Account** button is clicked

4 In the **Manage Your Account** dialog box, click the description on the right that most suits your need for help — the **Frequently Asked Questions** description in this example

(1) Logon to CompuServe

(2) Choose **Help↳Support Centre** to access **Member Services**

(3) Click a button or description

Again, click a button or description (4)

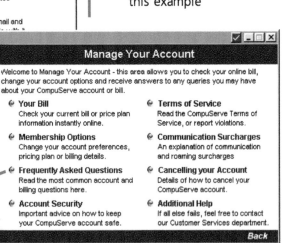

5 Locate the question you want to look at in the list, and double-click it to view it

OR:

6 Select another category to view the **Frequently Asked Questions** in that category

OR:

7 Click the **Search** button in any of the **Member Services** suite of dialog boxes to access a search of all online files

8 Click the description on the right side of the search you want to make

At any point in your online look for help, you can get back to the normal view of CompuServe by clicking either CompuServe 2000's **Main Menu** toolbar button, or simply clicking here

6 Click an alternate category

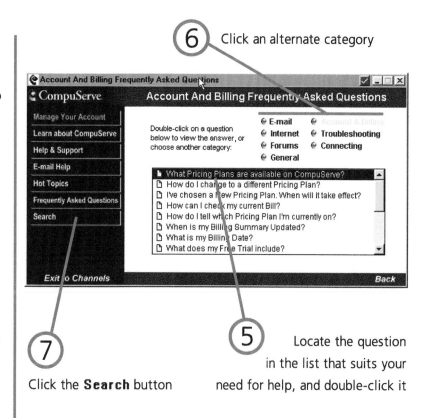

5 Locate the question in the list that suits your need for help, and double-click it

7 Click the **Search** button

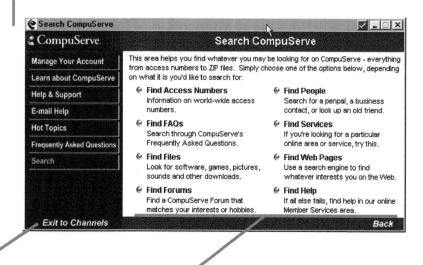

8 Click the description that most suits your need for help

Summary for Section 1

CompuServe is an online Internet service — featuring the best of the two worlds of an online service and the Internet.

CompuServe 2000 is the latest version of the CompuServe client software.

The **Main Menu** is the centre of CompuServe 2000 — you can reach any service on the CompuServe network from here.

You are logged onto the CompuServe service whenever all the toolbar buttons are active or a page is visible in the page area.

Use CompuServe's **GO** words to access services you want quickly.

Store frequently used **GO** words, as well as Internet URLs in your **Favourite Places**. This way they are accessible from the Favourite button on the toolbar.

Use CompuServe 2000's comprehensive in-built Help system to find out about all aspects of the program — use the CompuServe online help if further help is required.

2 Around the world in 80 mins

OK... Now what?

So you've logged onto CompuServe then logged back off again. You've used **GO** words once or twice, and you've seen and used the **Favourite Places** feature. But what's next? You've heard people talking about CompuServe as though it's immense (which, actually, it is) but so far you have no evidence that proves what it's really capable of.

That's the purpose of this section of this book. Over the next few pages you'll see an overview of what CompuServe is all about. You'll go places you never thought possible on your computer; you'll do the sorts of things you might previously have seen actors doing in spy films but never dreamed you can do on your own desktop; but what's best — it's all within the bounds of a familiar CompuServe interface. With just a click or two of your mouse button (and maybe just the odd bit of typing) you'll be able to visit all the services and use all the information here.

And what's more — this is still just the tip of CompuServe's iceberg. CompuServe grows daily, with new services and new features being added all the time, so knowing how to access it all is important. Start finding out here!

We start by looking at CompuServe 2000's main parts.

The toolbar

Many of the things you'll want to do regularly within CompuServe are available from a toolbar button. The toolbar's been arranged to hold the most popular services close to hand. We've seen the **Favourites** toolbar button (page 16) as the basis of Favourite Places, of course. Here we look at some others.

(page 16)

Tip:

Getting on the Internet when you're online with CompuServe is as easy as clicking a button — once you're there it's just as easy (because CompuServe and the Internet are vast) to get lost. To get back to the home ground of the familiar CompuServe 2000 display, just click the toolbar's Main Menu button. A brand new browser window will be created that displays CompuServe Today — the page that's always displayed when you first connect to CompuServe — as shown right.

While you're *within* the CompuServe service, on the other hand, clicking the main CompuServe logo (in the top-left corner of the browser window) also takes you straight back to the CompuServe Today page — this time, however, within the *same* browser window (whether it's re-sized, maximised or whatever)

Read Mail — one-click access to read new mail, old mail, or mail you have sent

Mail Centre — all mail features

Create Mail — one-click access to a new mail window

Favourite Places

People — communications features and services

Channels — drop-down menu access to CompuServe Channels

Features — drop-down menu access to popular services

Main Menu

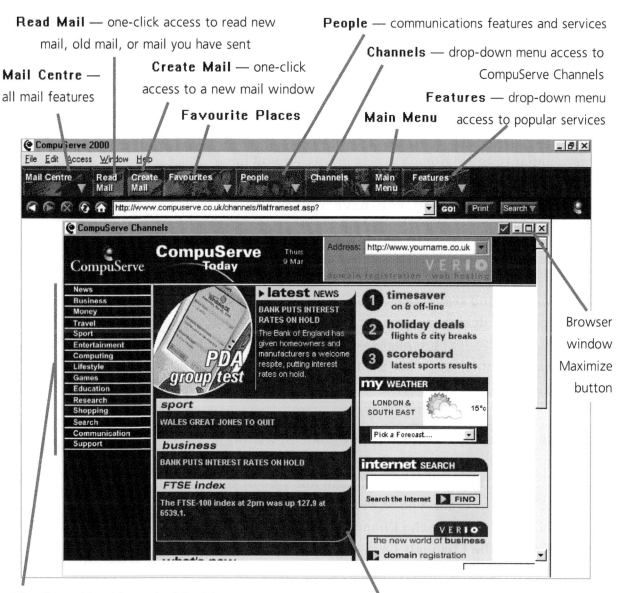

Browser window Maximize button

The Channel bar (down the left side of the browser) holds all the main Channels — see over the page.

The browser window — can be either a separate window (the default, as shown here) — or can be maximized to fill the browser area totally, becoming an integral part of the CompuServe 2000 display. Simply click the browser's Maximize button to do this

The Navigation bar

The Navigation bar controls the browser. Its main tools are:

Back   Stop loading   Home

Click **GO!** to go to the entry in the text field

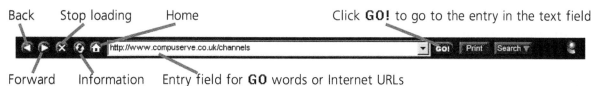

Forward   Information   Entry field for **GO** words or Internet URLs

Channels

The CompuServe service is so big, it's useful to think of it split up into several easy-to-access areas. These areas are called Channels — because they're actually very similar to television channels in use. As you have television channels dedicated to sport, or movies, or general programmes, so you have the equivalent CompuServe 2000 channels dedicated in the same way to various aspects of online life.

Channels are accessed from CompuServe 2000's in-built browser, and stepping from one to another can be as simple as clicking a hyperlink within a browser window. Over the next few pages we'll take a look at the Channels available, and what's on offer within.

Swimming the Channels

There are some 20+ Channels (at the time of writing), and more are in development. Many of these can be accessed from the Channels bar at the left side of the browser window. When you're viewing any particular Channel, you'll also see the Channel's menu structure opened out in the Channels bar.

All these Channels and their menus are hyperlinked — so often you can access the particular point in the system you want with a single click, or maybe two.

Apart from this, the Channels themselves (displayed in the rest of the browser window) may have hyperlinked areas that can be accessed in the same way, to jump you to other places — on *or* off the CompuServe service.

All in all, the whole Channels system is a complete and enjoyable interactive experience.

Basic steps:

1   Connect to the CompuServe service... err, that's it!

Take note:

The very first Channel you'll see is the one that CompuServe 2000 automatically goes to when you logon to the CompuServe network — it's called CompuServe Today. The content of CompuServe Today changes to reflect what's happening in the world on that day

Just to remind you, you can see when you're viewing a CompuServe Channel, because it tells you so in the browser window title bar

CompuServe Today — the very first channel you always see when you logon to CompuServe. The Channel reflects what's been happening on a daily basis, so is a useful starting point

① Logon

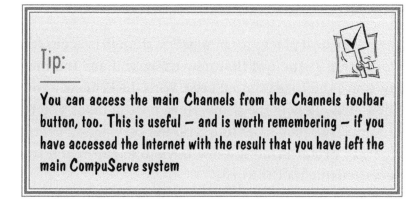

Main Channels on CompuServe are listed down the side of the browser window in the Channels bar. If you click a Channel, the browser will jump to that Channel, and the Channel's menu structure will open out in the Channels bar

Just as in Internet Web pages (see page 63), Channel pages have dedicated areas that link to other pages (these dedicated areas are called hyperlinks). You simply have to click a hyperlink to jump to that other page

Tip:

You can access the main Channels from the Channels toolbar button, too. This is useful – and is worth remembering – if you have accessed the Internet with the result that you have left the main CompuServe system

31

Welcome

The Welcome Channel is a useful stopping off point for new CompuServe users, and gives much important information, tips and hints for new users.

Basic steps:

1 Choose **Channels** ↦ **Welcome**, or **GO Welcome**

2 Click Ernie's **Click Here** button, or GO Get started

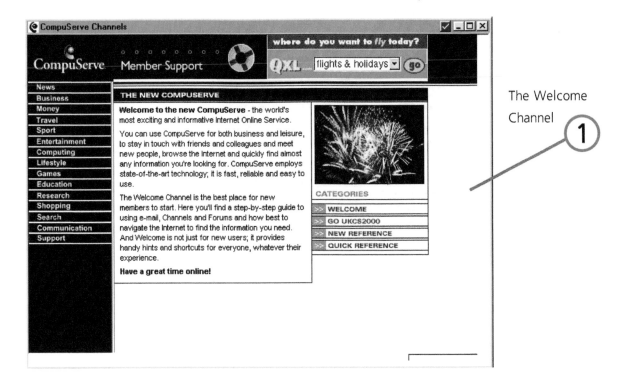

The Welcome Channel ①

Ernie

One of the best places for new users, though is accessed from Ernie — the owl that new users will see the first few times they use CompuServe. With the Ernie window open, just clicking the **Click Here** button takes you to CompuServe 2000's **Getting Started** service. All users, whether or not Ernie the owl is visible, can reach the service using its GO word.

New users click here to reach the **Getting Started** service, otherwise **GO Get started** ②

When you are in the Getting Started service, you can choose the area you want information on — here we are linking to information about Channels

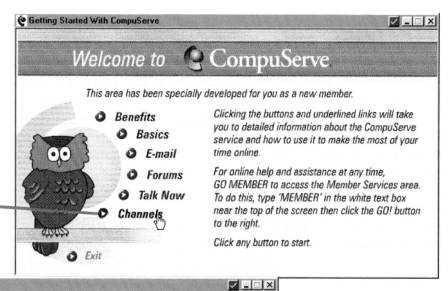

Within the Channel information area of Getting Started, there are various options — here we want information about using them

The information we want

Information can be printed for later reference, by clicking here

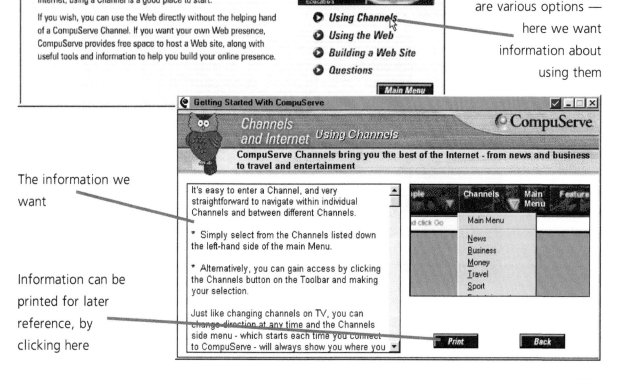

News

The **News** Channel contains — as you might expect — sections for national and international news, sport, business, entertainments, travel, weather, and so on.

The **News** Channel is the first Channel we've looked at that provides an opened out menu selection in the Channels bar. As such, it provides us with the opportunity to see how to use other Channels listed in the Channels bar.

Once in the Channel of your choice, you click subsections in the Channels bar, or click hyperlinked items on the page.

Basic steps:

1 Click the **News** button in the Channels bar, or **GO News**

2 Click the **Archive** subsection

3 Click the **World** subsection

Click **News**

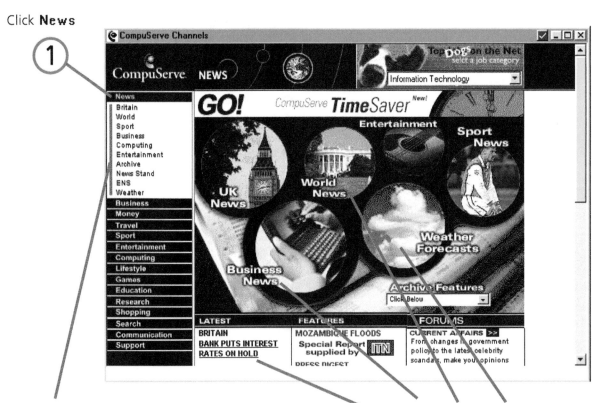

Click a section within the Channel you are in, to access that section's page

Click hyperlinked page content to access that content's page

34

7 Days news service — accessed by clicking the **Archive** subsection — is a service that allows you to filter recent news (although it's called 7 Days, you can specify any recent period)

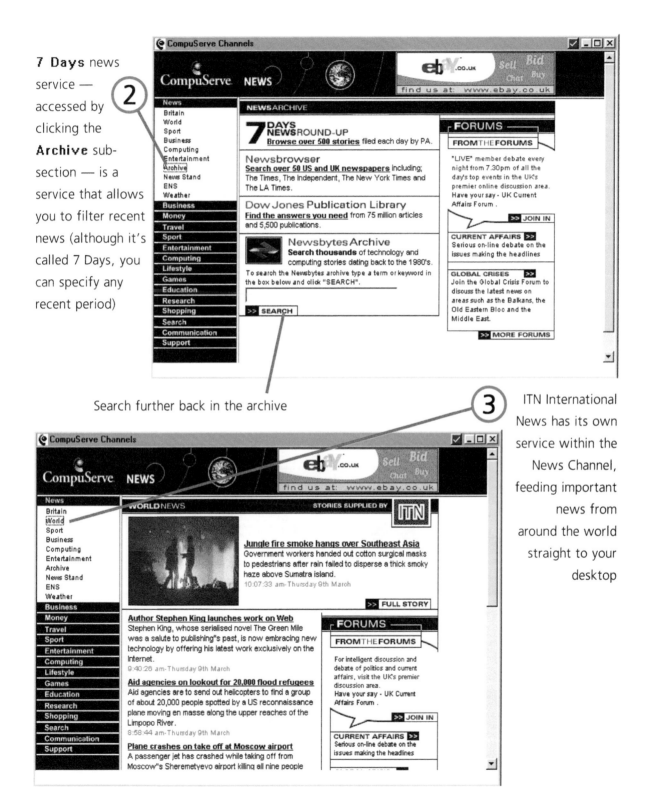

Search further back in the archive

ITN International News has its own service within the News Channel, feeding important news from around the world straight to your desktop

Business

Business and professional users are catered for with their own Channel. However, it's not exclusive to business and professional users (neither is the rest of CompuServe out of bounds to them, of course).

There's plenty of information and absolute mounds of services in the **Business** Channel to keep everybody happy on financial matters. Need information on companies? You can get company reports in a few clicks of your mouse's button.

Basic steps:

1 Click the **Business** Channel

2 Click the **Company Reports** sub-section, then click the **ICB Company Reports** hyperlink

3 From step 1, click the **Equifax** hyperlink

The **Business** Channel

36

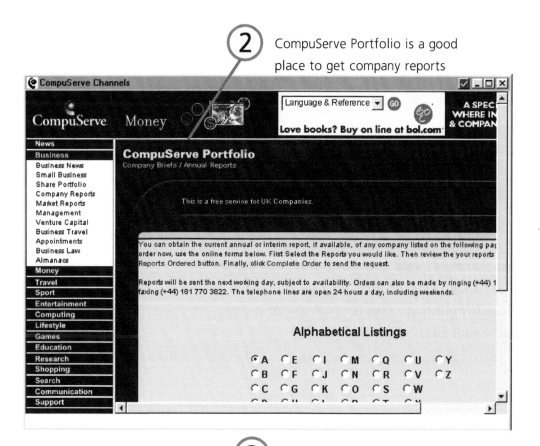

② CompuServe Portfolio is a good place to get company reports

③ Equifax

Equifax lets you locate company reports or directors

Money

Your money's in safe hands with CompuServe. Well, that is, if you use the CompuServe **Money** Channel, where you find all the latest news about investing, mortgages, savings, borrowing, exchange rates, shares and insurance.

Of particular notes in this Channel are the CompuServe Share Portfolio service, where you can keep a close track of all your shares, and the online access to a growing number of insurance companies — where you can obtain online premium quotes for just about every type of insurance you care to name.

Basic steps:

1 Click the **Money** Channel button in the Channels bar, or **GO Money**

2 Click the **Share Portfolio** hyperlink

3 Click the **Insurance** subsection

1 The **Money** Channel

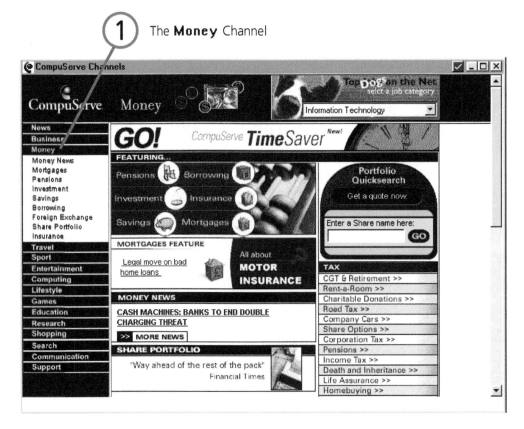

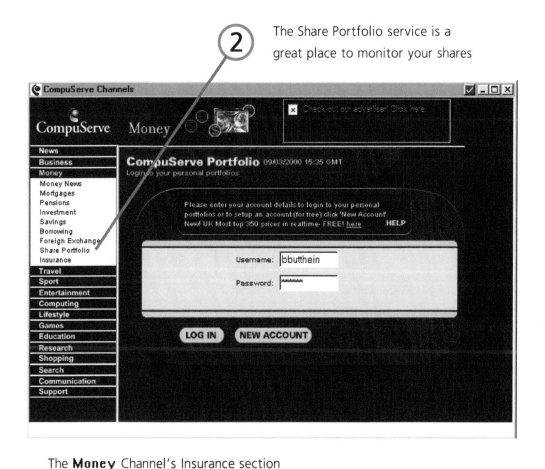

The Share Portfolio service is a great place to monitor your shares

The **Money** Channel's Insurance section

Online access to insurance companies means you can set up your insurance using CompuServe

Travel

Whoever you are, it's a safe bet that you'll travel from time to time.

Whether it's by train to work, or by plane on your holidays, or even by car to do the shopping, it's all travel. CompuServe 2000 has an extensive array of services, providing a great deal of information, that can help you:

▷ plan your route

▷ check your train timetable and itinerary

▷ and even book tickets online.

This and much more is available on the **Travel** Channel.

Basic steps:

1 Click the **Travel** Channel button in the Channels bar

2 Click the **Rail** sub-section

3 Click the **Air** sub-section, for flight information

1 The **Travel** Channel

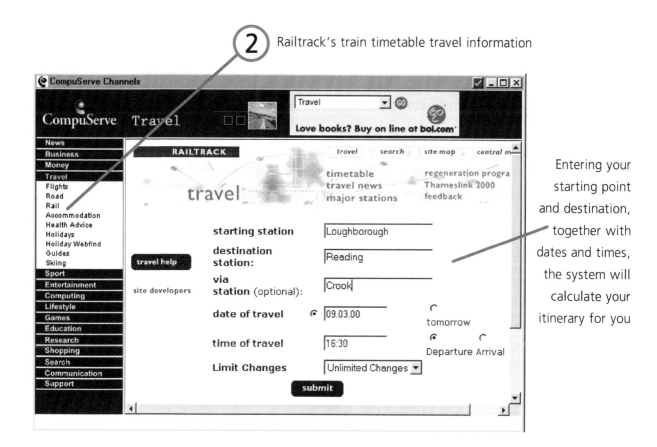

② Railtrack's train timetable travel information

Entering your starting point and destination, together with dates and times, the system will calculate your itinerary for you

Get all air related information by clicking the **Flights** sub-section

Sport

Of course, it goes without saying that CompuServe will have a Sport Channel. It holds almost everything you could hope to find about worldwide, UK and local sport, too. From international cricket results, downloadable golf utilities, and even sports quizzes — it's all there for the asking.

Take note:

The Sports Results service is accessible most easily from the Features menu in the toolbar – it is still a Channels service though

Basic steps:

1 Click the **Sport** Channel button in the Channels bar, or **GO Sport**

2 Click the **Sports News** sub-section in the **Sport** Channel

3 Choose **Features⤷Sports Results**

(1) The **Sport** Channel

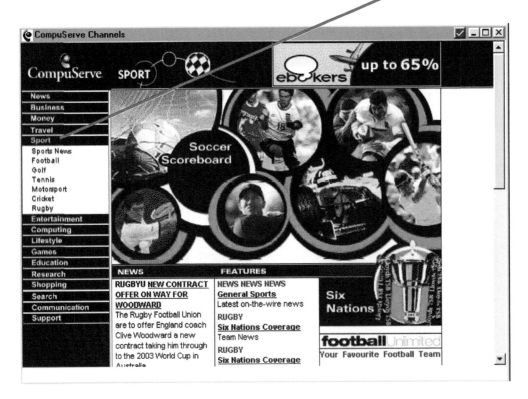

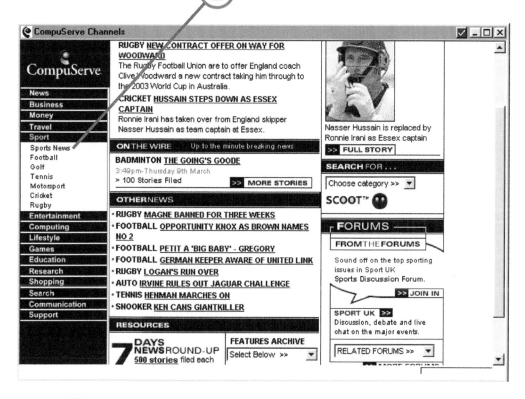

2 Sports News is a rolling newsfeed, that's updated regularly

CompuServe Channels

CompuServe

News
Business
Money
Travel
Sport
  Sports News
  Football
  Golf
  Tennis
  Motorsport
  Cricket
  Rugby
Entertainment
Computing
Lifestyle
Games
Education
Research
Shopping
Search
Communication
Support

RUGBY NEW CONTRACT OFFER ON WAY FOR WOODWARD
The Rugby Football Union are to offer England coach Clive Woodward a new contract taking him through to the 2003 World Cup in Australia.

CRICKET HUSSAIN STEPS DOWN AS ESSEX CAPTAIN
Ronnie Irani has taken over from England skipper Nasser Hussain as team captain at Essex.

ON THE WIRE   Up to the minute breaking news

BADMINTON THE GOING'S GOODE
3:49pm- Thursday 9th March
> 100 Stories Filed   **>> MORE STORIES**

OTHER NEWS

· **RUGBY** MAGNE BANNED FOR THREE WEEKS
· **FOOTBALL** OPPORTUNITY KNOX AS BROWN NAMES NO 2
· **FOOTBALL** PETIT A 'BIG BABY' - GREGORY
· **FOOTBALL** GERMAN KEEPER AWARE OF UNITED LINK
· **RUGBY** LOGAN'S RUN OVER
· **AUTO** IRVINE RULES OUT JAGUAR CHALLENGE
· **TENNIS** HENMAN MARCHES ON
· **SNOOKER** KEN CANS GIANTKILLER

RESOURCES

7 DAYS NEWS ROUND-UP
500 stories filed each

FEATURES ARCHIVE
Select Below >>

Nasser Hussain is replaced by Ronnie Irani as Essex captain
>> FULL STORY

SEARCH FOR . . .
Choose category >>
SCOOT™

FORUMS

FROM THE **FORUMS**
Sound off on the top sporting issues in Sport UK
Sports Discussion Forum.
>> JOIN IN

SPORT UK >>
Discussion, debate and live chat on the major events.

RELATED FORUMS >>

3

The **Sports Results** service lists results as they come in

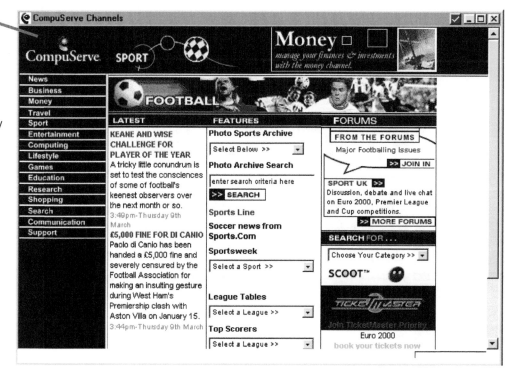

CompuServe Channels

CompuServe   SPORT

Money □ □
manage your finances & investments with the money channel.

News
Business
Money
Travel
Sport
Entertainment
Computing
Lifestyle
Games
Education
Research
Shopping
Search
Communication
Support

FOOTBALL

LATEST

KEANE AND WISE CHALLENGE FOR PLAYER OF THE YEAR
A tricky little conundrum is set to test the consciences of some of football's keenest observers over the next month or so.
3:49pm- Thursday 9th March

£5,000 FINE FOR DI CANIO
Paolo di Canio has been handed a £5,000 fine and severely censured by the Football Association for making an insulting gesture during West Ham's Premiership clash with Aston Villa on January 15.
3:44pm- Thursday 9th March

FEATURES

Photo Sports Archive
Select Below >>

Photo Archive Search
enter search criteria here
>> SEARCH

Sports Line

Soccer news from Sports.Com

Sportsweek
Select a Sport >>

League Tables
Select a League >>

Top Scorers
Select a League >>

FORUMS

FROM THE FORUMS
Major Footballing Issues
>> JOIN IN

SPORT UK >>
Discussion, debate and live chat on Euro 2000, Premier League and Cup competitions.
>> MORE FORUMS

SEARCH FOR . . .
Choose Your Category >>
SCOOT™

TICKET MASTER
Join TicketMaster Priority
Euro 2000
book your tickets now

Entertainment

The **Entertainment** Channel is the CompuServe centre for the worlds of the arts, movies, music, television, radio and media.

It's the place to go when you want to find out which bands are gigging round your 'hood, what's on the telly, what flicks are at the local fleapit, or what's on at a theatre near you.

Basic steps:

1 Click the **Entertainment** button in the Channels bar, or **GO Entertainment**

2 Click the **Latest News from the NME** hyperlink

3 Click the **TV** sub-section on the Channels bar

(1) The **Entertainment** Channel

(2) Click here

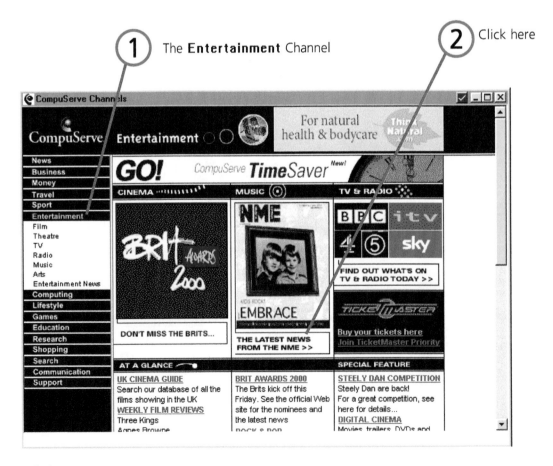

The NME section is a great way to keep up with modern music

Locate local gigs

Checkout the news

2 Listings for all television channels are on the Entertainment Channel

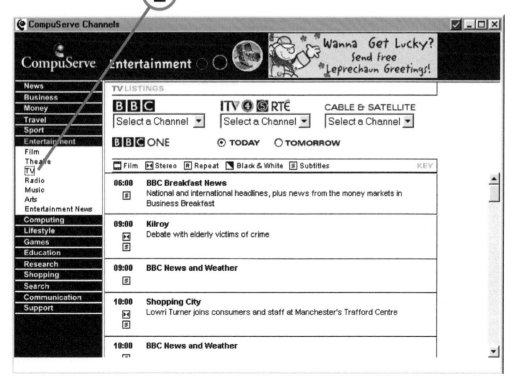

Computing

If you're using CompuServe, it's a safe bet you'll be doing so from a computer. It's a safe bet too, that you'll be interested in other matters to do with computers. With that in mind, CompuServe's **Computing** Channel is the place to go.

In the Computing Channel you'll find links to files, programs, news, references and support — in fact, more than likely everything you could ever possibly want in computing terms.

Basic steps:

1   Click the **Computing** button in the Channels bar, or **GO Computing**

2   Click the sub-section or link you need to access further information

The **Computing** Channel

Click a sub-section or link

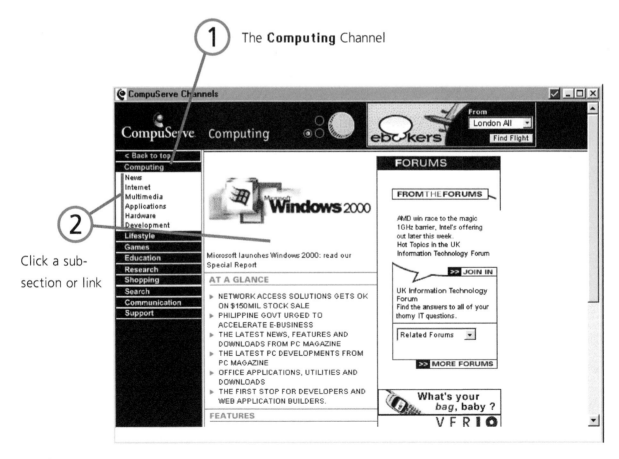

46

Basic steps:

1 Click the **Lifestyle** button in the Channels bar, or **GO Lifestyle**

2 Click the **Gardening** sub-section

3 Click the **Women** sub-section to view the Women's Channel

Lifestyle

CompuServe 2000's Lifestyle channel is the place for you, your home, your family, your hobbies, your health, and well, yes, your lifestyle.

Sub-sections within the Lifestyle channel reflect some of the most important aspects of CompuServe users' lives, and linked areas within Channel sub-sections help to centralise content so that everything is within just a couple of mouse clicks.

If you want a review of the latest Model-T with go-faster stripes, or you need to locate propagation details for Lonicera Fragrantissima (*honeysuckle* to you and me) then the Lifestyle Channel's the place to look.

① The Lifestyle Channel

Click **Gardening**

Click **Women**

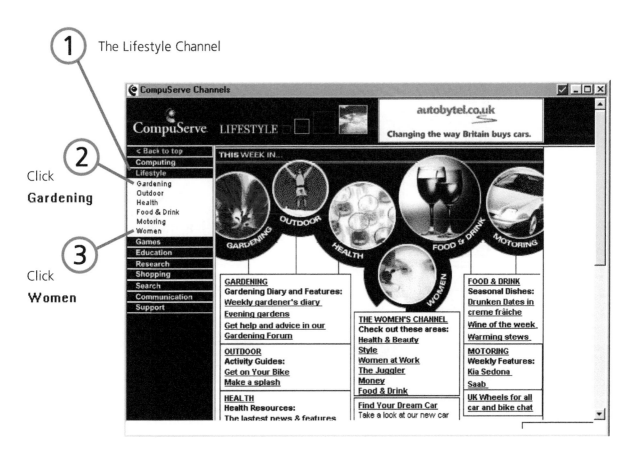

Lifestyle (contd)

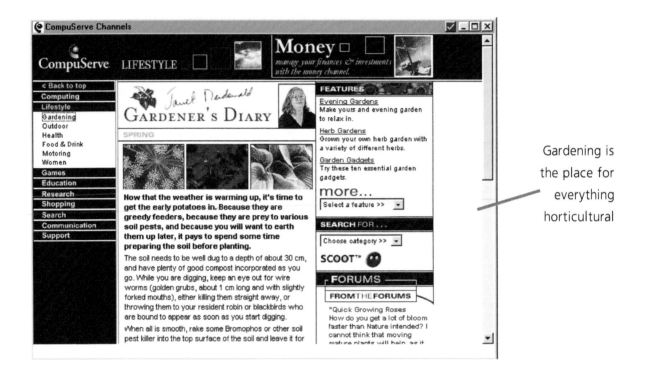

Gardening is the place for everything horticultural

The Women's Channel

Games

1   Click the **Games** button
    on the CompuServe
    Channels bar, or **GO
    Games**

2   Play!

You wouldn't be a *real* computer user if you didn't play computer games, would you? CompuServe's **Games** Channel is your source for the computer games world and all to do with it.

You can pit your wits against others in Internet-wide games, and you can download games to your own computer. You can see what the gamers' charts are like, and you can join in discussions about whether games consoles are superior to personal computers for playing games.

It really doesn't matter what sort of games you like playing, there's news, reviews and links about them all.

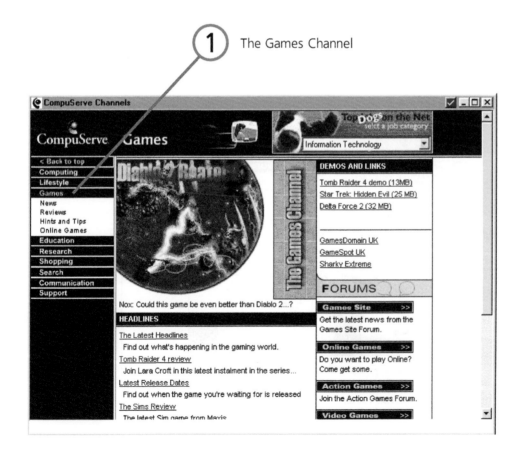

The Games Channel

Education

Whether you're a parent, teacher, manager or student, there's a wealth of information in the **Education** Channel.

Whether it's educational software you want for your computer, links to school Web sites, advice from the Government, how to apply to go to University, careers services, or even how to checkout the Encyclopaedias online, the **Education** Channel will be able to help you out.

Basic steps:

1 Click the **Education** button in the Channels bar, or **GO Education**

2 Click the **Study** sub-section on the Education Channel bar

3 Click the **Parents** sub-section, to locate advice on choosing schools

(1) The **Education** Channel

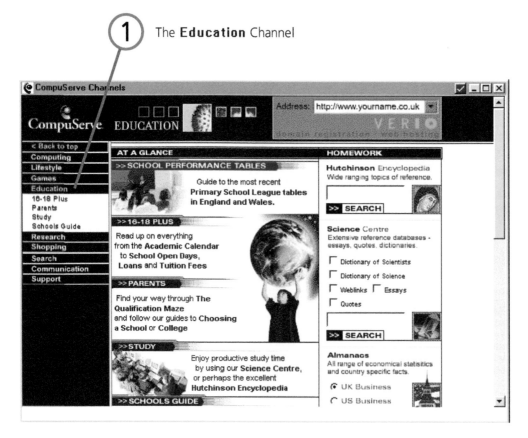

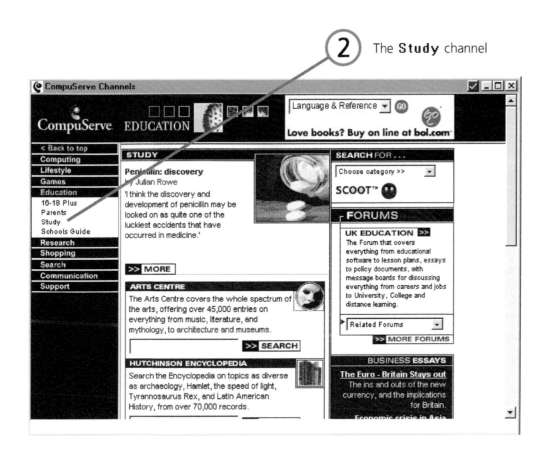

2 The **Study** channel

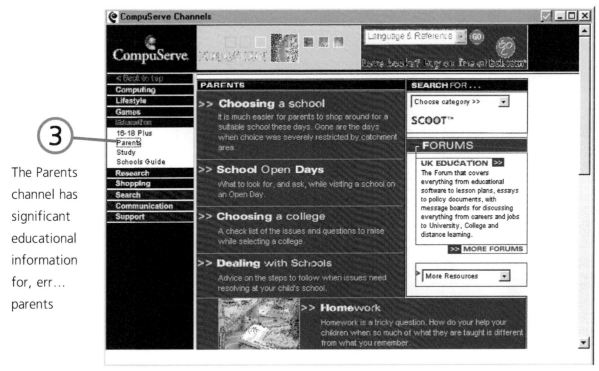

The Parents channel has significant educational information for, err... parents

3

Research

One of the most important uses of an online service such as CompuServe is as a resource for information. CompuServe's **Research** Channel is the place you need to go for any information: whether you want merely to check the spelling of a word, or find a map of a city you're about to visit, or see what your local museum is charging for admission.

Here are some good examples of how the **Research** Channel can be used as a valuable online reference library to locate UK business information and global economy details.

Basic steps:

1 Click the **Research** button of the Channels bar

2 Click the **Almanacs** sub-section

3 Click the **Sci-Tech** sub-section

(1) The **Research** Channel

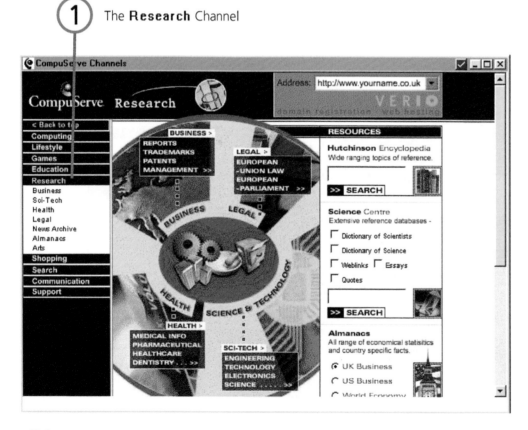

(2) The **Almanacs** channel — the place to locate important information of companies in the UK or elsewhere

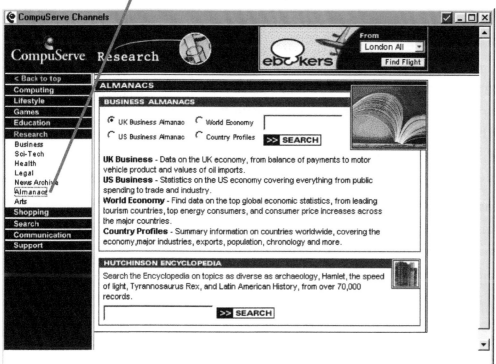

The Science and Technology service

(3)

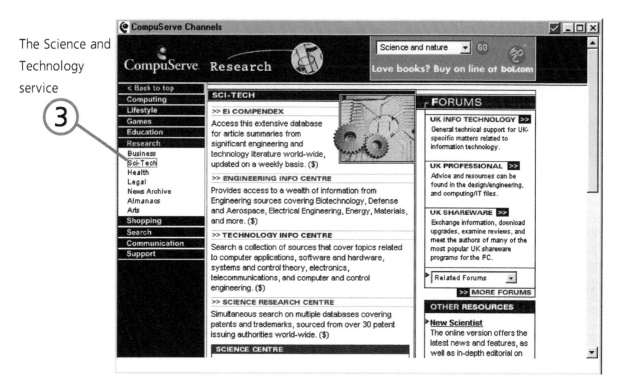

Shopping

Basic steps:

1 Click the **Shopping** button on the CompuServe Channel bar

2 Click the **Auctions** sub-section

3 Click the **Music & Video** sub-section

Forget the trudge to the shops. Forget parking, the traffic, the fumes, the crowds, the queues, and the unpacking. We've already seen how you can book aeroplane flights over the Internet. Now CompuServe has teamed up with several partners in the retail industry, to provide an online shopping service that's simply second-to-none.

By using CompuServe's **Shopping** Channel you could possibly never have to set foot over your doorstep again — if you didn't want to, that is.

GO on! Live a hermit's life...

...do it all with CompuServe 2000!

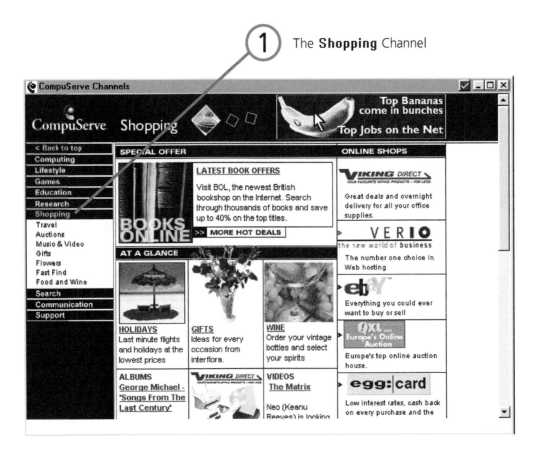

① The **Shopping** Channel

② CompuServe's Auctions service is a great place to buy and sell

③ Shop online for your music and video needs

Weather

Yes, that's right...

   ... weather or not it's going to rain!

CompuServe 2000's rapid response to data is the ideal thing when it comes to providing you with up-to-the-minute weather information.

While it *is* a Channel in its own right, because it's such a frequented service, it's accessible right from the **Features** menu in the toolbar — always to hand.

What's more — you can tailor the weather report you view on-screen to suit yourself. Tell the service what cities and regions you want to be included, and the service does the rest for you, automatically.

Basic steps:

1 Choose **Features⤷ Latest Weather**, or **GO Weather**

2 That's it!

1 UK weather — from the **Weather** Channel

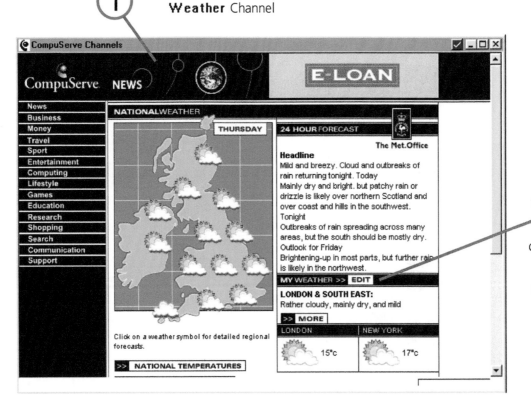

Click here, then choose your own details to be included in the weather report

56

Member Support

1   Click the **Support**
    channel

2   Click the sub-section or
    link you need to access
    further information

We looked at CompuServe 2000's in-built and online help systems in the previous section. However, help with individual aspects of CompuServe 2000 is only one side of the coin. The flip side is the general support that members have — simply because they *are* members.

All this support offered by CompuServe is centred around the Member Support Channel. It's here where you'll find the information you might need to maintain your account.

If you are having general problems, or need information about your account, or want to know how to change other aspects, it's to the Member Support Channel you should turn first.

(1)   The **Member Support** Channel

Click the sub-
section or
hyperlink you
want

(2)

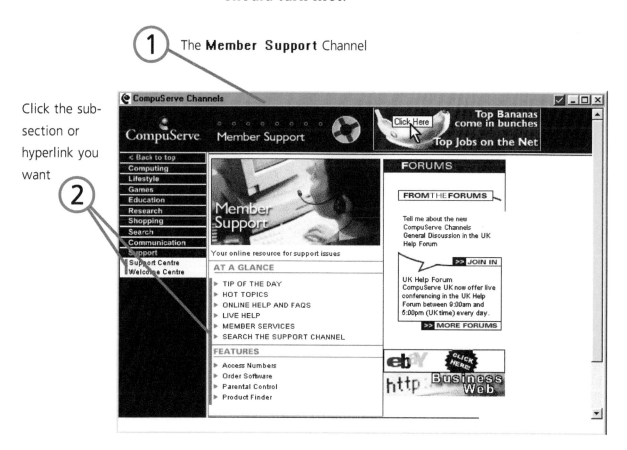

Summary for Section 2

Use toolbar buttons for rapid access to often-used services within CompuServe.

Channels are the central way of life in CompuServe 2000. Whatever your interests, there'll be Channels that you can use.

There are currently around 20 Channels, mostly arranged down the Channels bar at the left side of the CompuServe 2000 browser.

Beginners to CompuServe, and users still unfamiliar with the new CompuServe 2000 client interface, should **GO Welcome**. This takes you to the Welcome Channel. Better still, **Go Get started** to see Ernie the owl's **Getting Started** service.

Channels are often interlinked — you might find yourself jumping from one Channel to another if you access a service that refers (with a hyperlink) to a service which is in another Channel.

3 The Internet

What is the Internet?

There's a lot said about the Internet; but what is it?

The Internet is — very simply — a collection of computers around the world. These computers are all linked together, so that information on one computer can easily pass to another computer. To ensure this, a standard set of Internet rules (called *protocols*) is used which controls the transfer of data between connected computers (known, as a result, as *transfer control protocols/Internet protocols* — TCP/IP). Computers of any type, operating system, and capability can be on the Internet, as long as they use TCP/IP.

Usually, individuals' computers (that is, yours and mine) aren't connected directly on the Internet. Instead, our computers connect using an Internet service provider (such as CompuServe), which provides a sort of socket in the Internet into which we plug our computers — using a modem and telephone line.

There are many facets to a worldwide computer network like the Internet — the most important being e-mail and the World Wide Web.

E-mail enables rapid text communications between Internet users. We look at it in the next section.

The World Wide Web has its own set of protocols (*hypertext markup language* — HTML) which allows Internet users to create Web sites, which other Internet users can access. On a Web site, Web pages are stored. Other Internet users can look at Web pages on a Web site with a program known as a Web browser. The browser in CompuServe 2000 installed on your computer is actually a Web browser (as if by chance), so straight away you can access the World Wide Web.

Take note:

Web pages usually contain text *and* images, stored in HTML format, so that when your Web browser accesses the page, you see displayed on your screen more-or-less what the site creator had on screen when the page was designed.

Also on Web pages (and this is the clever bit) can be hyperlinks – references to other places on the Internet – which a Web browser jumps to when you click them. This leads to one of the most fascinating things about the Internet – jumping (commonly called *surfing*) from Web site to Web site around the world as the information and your whim takes you

So where's my surfboard?

Tip:

As of the next page or so, you'll be popping around the Internet CompuServe 2000-style. As you do though, remember to save Web pages you visit and may want to visit again in your Favourite Places (see pages 16–19).

Re-visiting them is then a simple matter of choosing them from the Favourites menu on the toolbar

We've said all along that CompuServe is an online service that operates on the Internet. As a result, it has two sides to its use:

▷ the CompuServe 2000 interface, where you access all of CompuServe's online services

▷ an integrated Web browser, where you access the Internet.

These are highly integrated and you have already used both: having already been on the Internet (possibly without realising) if you've followed the examples and steps covered so far — because CompuServe Channels are all Web-based. In other words, the CompuServe network uses standard HTML protocols for all of its pages.

Having said that, Channels are still within the sheltered environment of the CompuServe network. Hyperlinks on Channel pages most usually refer to other CompuServe services or other Channels, the whole visual effect is of a more-or-less united appearance, and the things you see are tightly defined by CompuServe. You have to be a CompuServe member to access the online services, and you don't have to step outside CompuServe if you don't want to.

The Internet outside CompuServe, on the other hand, is less well-defined — it's a bit of a free-for-all, actually. Hyperlinks there can (and do) take you anywhere — you can be perusing the Natural History Museum in London's Web site and notice a hyperlink to the Louvre in Paris. Clicking the hyperlink takes you straight there. Inevitably, you end up looking at a Web site far removed from where you started.

URLs

The hyperlinks on a Web page are URLs (uniform resource locators). URLs are the Internet equivalent of longitude and latitude map references, which locate any particular point on the earth's surface.

A URL such as: `http://www.compuserve.co.uk` uniquely locates a particular 'place' on the Internet, just as 'step out the back door, turn left and take six steps' uniquely locates the rhubarb in my garden.

We can break down a URL into its constituent parts to see what it all means:

▷ `http://` — means that it refers to *hypertext transfer protocol* (this is the protocol used by the World Wide Web). This indicates that the following parts of the URL will locate a Web site on the World Wide Web. There are other protocol indicators — see the Tip on the right

▷ `www` — is a common URL part that also identifies the URL as pointing to the World Wide Web. It's a very common part of World Wide Web URLs, although by no means essential

▷ `compuserve` — the central part of the URL, indicating who the Web site belongs to (CompuServe, in this example)

▷ `co` — (`com` in the US) indicates that the Web site belongs to a company rather than an academic institution — `ac` in the UK, or `edu` in the US — say, or a government — `gov`

▷ `uk` — the Web site is in the UK. US Web sites don't have a country identifier, but every other country does.

You'll find URLs to surf to almost everywhere these days: magazines, newspapers, adverts, business cards and so on.

Tip:

The first part of a URL indicates the protocol that is used to access the computer (usually called a server) you connect to. There are several protocols, including these, although — unless you're an Internet 'power' user — you'll probably only come across the first three or, maybe, four:

▷ `http://` – hypertext transfer protocol (the World Wide Web)

▷ `mailto:` – Internet e-mail protocol

▷ `ftp://` – file transfer protocol, commonly used to access file libraries on the Internet

▷ `news:` – a site where subject-based news is available

▷ `telnet://` – a method of controlling one computer with another

▷ `file://` – denotes that the document is held on the computer you're using

Web browsing

1   Click anywhere in the **GO** text field on the CompuServe 2000 navigation bar

2   Enter the URL: `http://www.compuserve.co.uk.`

3   Click the **GO!** button

If you have a Web site URL, the easiest way to access it is to GO there, using CompuServe 2000's in-built GO system. As an example, we'll use CompuServe's own Web site, accessible by anyone from the Internet.

Take note:

When you're entering a URL, it's very important to get it right. Type it exactly as you see it — with no spaces, with dots not commas, with slashes in the right direction, and spelt in exactly the same way

Enter URL

Click **GO!**

(2)

(3)

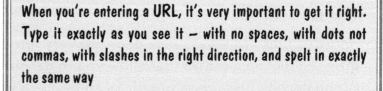

(1)

Click here

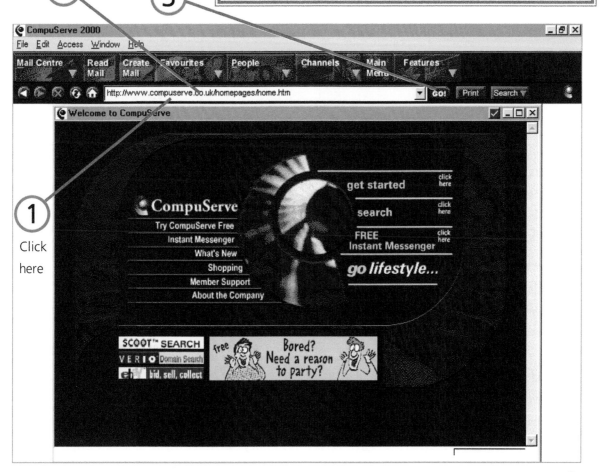

File transfers

One of the main features of the Internet is that you can access and download files from all around the world. Information and computer programs can be supplied this way to any Internet user. In effect, the Internet, and in particular the World Wide Web, has become the largest store of information and computer files in the world — simply because it *encompasses* the world, and is available to everyone *in* the world with an Internet connection!

Downloaded files are always encoded, and very often compressed too. So, utilities that allow you to decompress and decode files are required. As an example of downloading, here's how to download a free utility, which can decode and decompress most file encoding or compression formats, so is a useful tool to have.

Basic steps:

1 In the navigation bar field enter the URL: http:// www.aladdinsys.com

2 Click the **GO!** button

3 Follow the hyperlink on the Aladdin Systems Web site home page to the Aladdin Expander download page

4 Provide the information requested, then click the relevant hyperlinks to download Aladdin Expander. The utility is downloaded to your computer

Tip:

Downloads using your Web browser are usually set to download into the Download folder, inside the CompuServe 2000 folder on your hard disk.

You can, however, set the browser preferences to download files elsewhere, say, directly onto your computer desktop. This makes it easier to locate the files once downloaded. Choose Access↪Preferences, then click the Download icon. In the Download Preferences dialog box, set your preferred download folder

Tip:

Treat Internet URLs as GO words — enter them directly into either a GO Word dialog box, or (better) straight into the text field of the navigation bar. So steps 1 & 2 above could be simplified to:

GO http://www.aladdinsys.com

We'll use them as GO words from now on

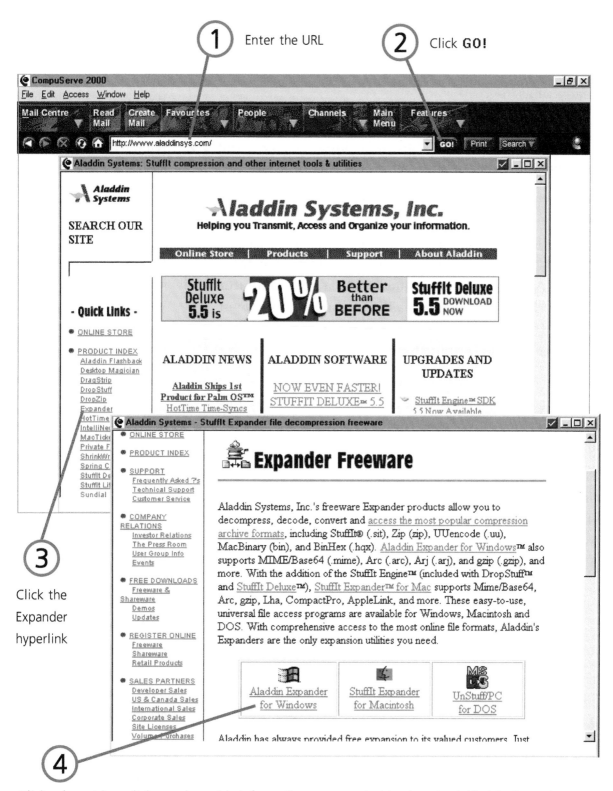

① Enter the URL

② Click **GO!**

③ Click the Expander hyperlink

④ Click relevant hyperlinks, and provide information as requested to download Aladdin Expander

PDF files...

Peedy what files?

PDFs (portable document format) are specially created files that can be viewed, read and printed on any of the main computer platforms (Windows, MacOS, Unix).

Files created as PDFs contain all the information necessary to view, read and print within themselves. In other words, all formatting, typestyles and graphics included in the original creation are held in electronic form within. As such, it doesn't matter that the computer used to view, read and print a PDF document hasn't got the particular fonts or styles, or formats, or graphics — they are all held within the bounds of the document itself.

All that's necessary is for the computer user who wishes to open a PDF is to have the respective PDF viewing application on the computer.

There are — as you might expect — several PDF variations. However, the one format that has become the standard for use with the Internet (and for many other purposes too — user manuals for software, for example, are often distributed in this format) is Adobe's Acrobat format. Wherever you surf on the Internet there's a good chance you'll find downloadable files that are stored in the Acrobat format (even the Inland Revenue Web site, at: http://www.open.gov.uk/inrev/irleaf2.htm has PDF files of some of its leaflets regarding income tax you can download).

If you haven't already got an Acrobat viewer program on your computer (or if you haven't got the latest version — version 4 at the time of writing) then here is how to get your very own copy.

Basic steps:

1 **GO** http://www.adobe.com

2 When the Adobe home page opens, click the **Get Acrobat Reader** button (probably located at the bottom of the page)

3 Follow the instructions on the **Download Acrobat Reader** page to download the Acrobat reader software for your computer

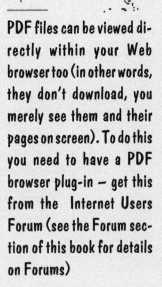

Tip:

PDF files can be viewed directly within your Web browser too (in other words, they don't download, you merely see them and their pages on screen). To do this you need to have a PDF browser plug-in — get this from the Internet Users Forum (see the Forum section of this book for details on Forums)

(1) Type the URL in the navigation
bar text field, then click **GO!**

The Adobe
Web page

(2) Click the **Get Acrobat Reader** button
located lower down the Web page

(3) Follow instructions
on later Web pages

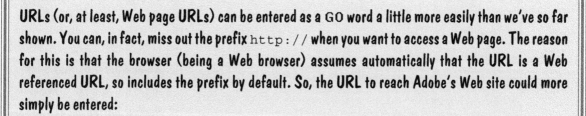

Tip:

URLs (or, at least, Web page URLs) can be entered as a GO word a little more easily than we've so far shown. You can, in fact, miss out the prefix `http://` when you want to access a Web page. The reason for this is that the browser (being a Web browser) assumes automatically that the URL is a Web referenced URL, so includes the prefix by default. So, the URL to reach Adobe's Web site could more simply be entered:

```
www.adobe.com
```

Searching

In our travels around the CompuServe network so far, we've really only used the Internet as a basis for CompuServe Channels. But, huge as the CompuServe network is (and believe me, it *is* huge!) the Internet itself is simply unthinkably big — and getting bigger by the day. Estimates of computers connected to the Internet vary (because it's impossible to state the number with any accuracy at all) but all agree that there are several million computer servers, all with many megabytes (if not gigabytes) of computer data available.

That poses a problem. If the Internet's so big, how can we possibly hope to find any particular information we want? The solution is in the form of *search engines*.

Think of a search engine as a librarian in a huge reference library. When you first enter a library, you ask the librarian where to find books on the topic you're interested in. The librarian tells you, and sends you off in the direction of the corresponding bookshelves for you to browse the books yourself.

CompuServe 2000's in-built search engine does just that — for information stored on the CompuServe network, as well as information stored on the Internet.

1 Click the **Search** Channel on the **Main Menu**

2 Type in the topic you want to find information on

3 Set the controls to define the search

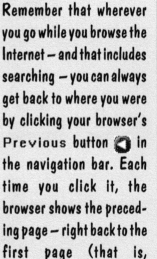

Tip:

Remember that wherever you go while you browse the Internet — and that includes searching — you can always get back to where you were by clicking your browser's **Previous** button in the navigation bar. Each time you click it, the browser shows the preceding page — right back to the first page (that is, CompuServe Today) in your current CompuServe session.

Remember also that clicking the Main Menu toolbar button takes you to CompuServe Today too

4 Click the **Find** button

5 In the search results, click a relevant hyperlink — the browser will jump to the URL referenced by the hyperlink

Enter a topic

②

Set the controls for your search. Here we've specified that the search should look for all words entered, and the search should be worldwide

③

Click **FIND**

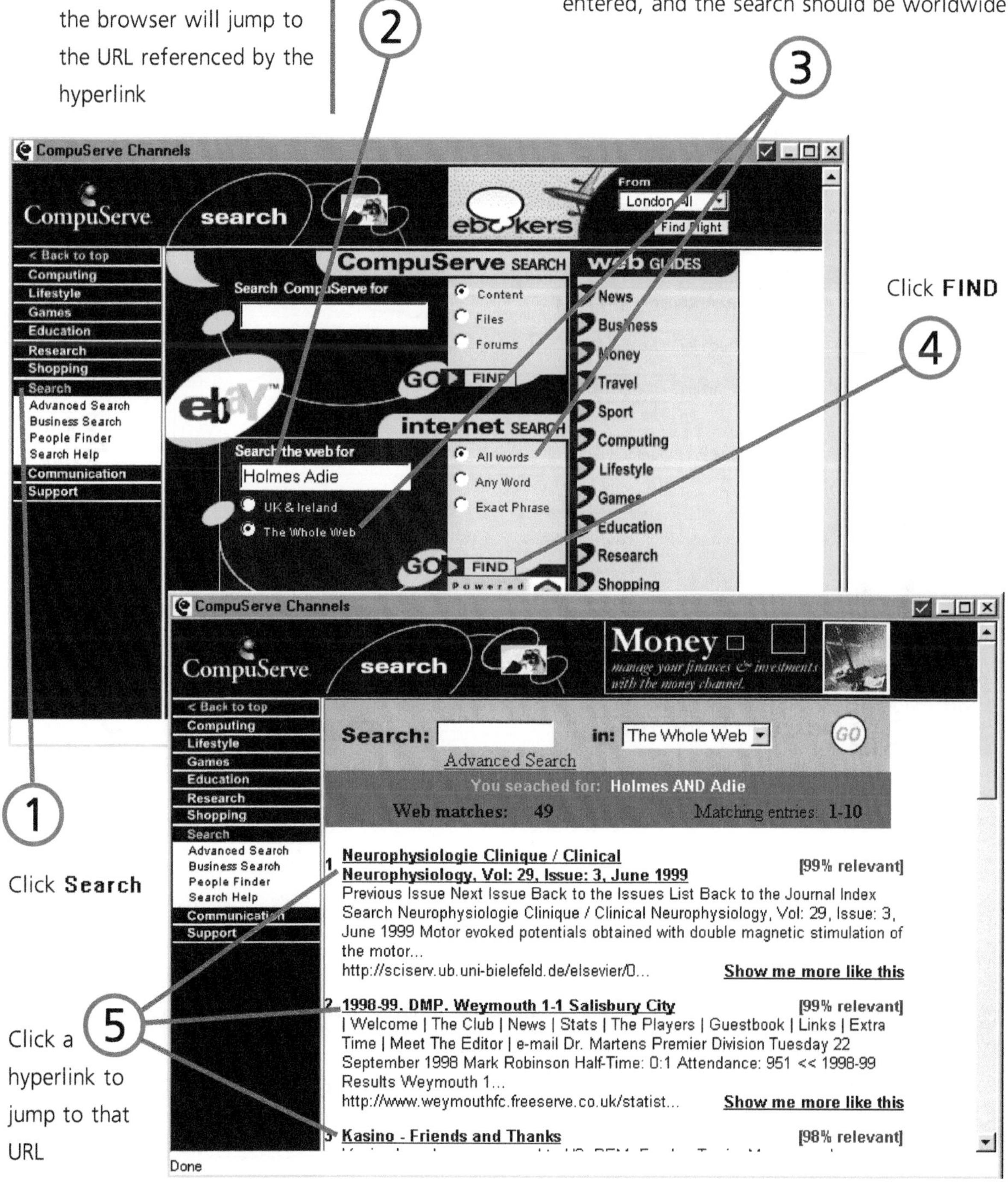

④

①

Click **Search**

⑤

Click a hyperlink to jump to that URL

Advanced searching

A search can result in many hyperlinks — particularly if you search for a broad topic. CompuServe 2000 offers the option of being able to refine searches by adding extra keywords or defining search methods.

Basic steps:

1 Click the **Advanced Search** sub-section

2 Type in the topic

3 Set the search controls

4 Click **Find**

Click **Advanced Search**

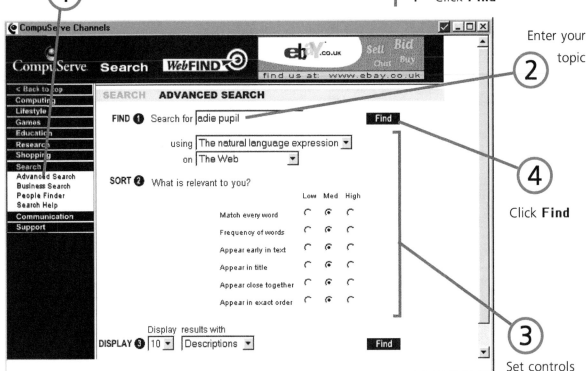

Enter your topic

Click **Find**

Click **Find**

Set controls

Tip:

Use controlling words (called operators) in your search:

▷ **OR – eg,** `adie or pupil`, **will locate instances of either word**

▷ **AND – eg,** `adie and pupil` **will locate both words**

▷ **AND NOT – eg,** `adie and not pupil`, **locates instance where adie is found but not pupil**

▷ **"" – eg,** `"adie pupil"` **will locate only those words together**

Basic steps:

1 Click the **Business Search** hyperlink

2 Enter the type of business you want to locate

3 Type in the location

4 Click the **Scoot** button

Business search

CompuServe 2000 also has an in-built means of locating business in the form of Scoot. The Scoot Web-based search engine provides the same information as its telephone-based system counterpart.

Enter the sort of business ②

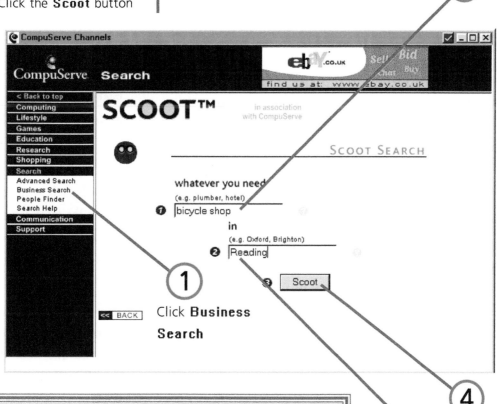

① Click **Business Search**

③ Enter the location you want

④ Click **Scoot**

Take note:

These are not the only search engines on the Internet – merely the default ones used by CompuServe. If neither locates information you want, try out another search engine, such as Alta Vista:

    GO www.altavista.com

File encoding

One of the attractions about the Internet is that computer files can be transmitted between computers. These files can be simple word processor or spreadsheet documents; email; or even computer programs.

The Internet allows this because the network relies on designated computers acting as *gateways* — analogous to postal mail sorting offices — taking in files then passing them on, in the process directing and re-directing them towards their destinations.

Internet gateways do this job only with text files. Files of other formats *might* work with gateways — but this can't be guaranteed. Basic computer files, on the other hand, are in *binary* format. So, to make sure files arrive at their destinations correctly, binary files are first converted to text form in a process called *encoding*.

Generally, this means two things for all Internet users — and as a CompuServe user, this includes you! First, files you receive from the Internet are encoded. They need to be *decoded* before your computer uses them. Second, any file you want to send over the Internet to other users must be encoded first.

In most instances, your Web browser is able to decode files received from the Internet (known as *downloading* — see page 64); while CompuServe 2000 itself decodes most files you receive and encodes files you want to send with mail (see page 104). Decoding usually occurs transparently, and you don't even know it's happened. For the few instances when both your Web browser and CompuServe 2000 can't cope, we recommend the free utility Aladdin Expander, which decodes most known encoded file formats — see page 65.

Take note:

Three common methods of encoding binary files into text files exist (although there *are* others).

While you use CompuServe and the Internet you might hear of these, so it's useful to know what they are and where they are commonly used:

▷ UUEncode — to date, this is the most common encoding method, simply because it's the oldest method around

▷ Base64 — the most recent encoding method, and the one now preferred. In time, this will be used for all Internet encoding purposes

▷ BinHex — common in the MacOS world (although also useful for Windows purposes, too) until Base64 came along

File compression

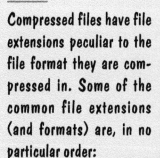

Tip:

Compressed files have file extensions peculiar to the file format they are compressed in. Some of the common file extensions (and formats) are, in no particular order:

▷ zip – the most common Windows format

▷ sit – Stuffit format files, the most common Macintosh format

▷ arj – Arj format

▷ arc – Arc format

▷ gzip – a Unix computer compression format

▷ sea – a self-expanding archive in Stuffit or similar format

▷ bin – MacBinary; another common MacOS compression format.

These are worth getting to know, as some decompression utilities handle some formats better than others. Note that Aladdin Expander handles them all

To save time when transmitting files (and, hence, save on your telephone bill) it's usual to compress files before transfer. Also, files you download (and files attached to email messages) are invariably compressed. Compression is regularly used on Internet and on-line service file archives simply to save space.

As when decoding received files (see opposite), your Web browser and CompuServe 2000 itself will help you decompress files compressed in common formats. But you may need extra utilities to compress files you want to send to other users, and you need utilities to decompress any files you receive which aren't in common compression format.

Common in the Windows world is the zip format. There are several zip utilities and most users will have access to at least one.

Common in the Macintosh world, however, is the Stuffit format, and if you receive a file that has been compressed in such a way, you will need a utility to decompress it. Fortunately, Aladdin Expander (the free utility suggested opposite — used for decoding binary files to text format) can also be used for decompression for Stuffit compressed files.

Of relevance to users is the fact that the Stuffit compression format (while being the main Mac format) *does* occur in Windows too, and it's worth downloading a copy of Aladdin Expander (see page 64) as a card-up-the-sleeve.

As well as decompressing Stuffit compressed files, Expander decompresses most other compression formats (including zip) too, so is a handy utility to have.

Summary for Section 3

Access the whole Internet from CompuServe 2000 — as well as the CompuServe service — in a seamless implementation. You can move easily from the CompuServe online service to the Internet and vice versa. In many cases you might not even realise you have changed from one to the other.

URLs (uniform resource locators) are the electronic equivalents of postal addresses. They are an absolute pointer to a file, a server, or a Web site or page, anywhere on the Internet, anywhere in the world.

Use CompuServe 2000's integrated Web browser to view Internet Web pages by entering a URL in the navigation bar field and clicking the **GO!** button.

Get the latest version of Adobe's free Acrobat viewer, so that you can view, read and print PDF files you download from the Internet.

Use CompuServe 2000's in-built search engines to find information on the Internet.

Locate and download Aladdin Expander — a free utility — to help in decoding and decompression of files you might download or receive attached to email messages.

4 Mail

What is mail?

One of CompuServe's best and most used features is the ability to send and receive electronic mail (e-mail) messages to anyone else in the world with an Internet connection. You do this from the CompuServe 2000 **Mail Centre**.

E-mail (called simply *mail* within CompuServe) really is just like ordinary mail (called *snailmail* by techies). You receive a mail message because it has your CompuServe address on it — just like an envelope has your postal address on it. You open it and read it just like opening a letter and reading it. You create your own mail to send just like writing a letter, you address it with the recipient's mail address, and finally you post it. All your actions within CompuServe mail are electronic — but the actions are merely the digital copies of postal mail.

CompuServe acts as a giant post office cum mailbox. You write your letter in the form of mail on your computer. When it's time to post it you logon to CompuServe and send it. The CompuServe network holds it (or passes it onto the network the recipient belongs to), until the person you addressed it to logs on to receive mail.

Being all electronic, CompuServe's mail process is quicker, cheaper, and ultimately simpler than the snailmail process.

Person sending snailmail puts their letter in an envelope, and writes an address on the envelope before posting it. An e-mail message is the same, except it's on-screen and has the recipient's e-mail — not postal — address

A snailmail letter is delivered through the postal system to the address on the envelope — the e-mail is merely held in the recipient's electronic mailbox until logging on

Take note:

Just like sending a snailmail letter, you need to have a person's correct mail address before you can send a mail message to that person, otherwise — just like a snailmail letter — it will bounce back to you, undelivered.

The problem is even more acute with incorrectly addressed e-mail than with incorrectly addressed snailmail because — while a human postperson can sometimes look at an snailmail address on an envelope and realise, perhaps, that "the Brindleys don't live at number 17 Brindley Mansions, they live at number 19", so get the right letter to the right recipient — electronic mail is delivered by computer postpersons... err, no, I mean computers, which can't do this, so they send the e-mail straight back (or deliver it to the wrong address)

Two mail methods

Generally there are two ways of handling mail within CompuServe 2000. First, you can handle all your incoming mail while you are online. This is how we suggest you do it initially, and is how the first part of this section has been written. Alternatively, you can opt to retrieve (that is, download from CompuServe to your computer) all incoming mail messages in a single operation (called a *schedule*). Scheduling is covered in the final part of the section (see *Sending mail later*, page 94).

As you might expect, there are benefits (and drawbacks) for both methods:

➤ working with mail online means you can delete those mail messages you don't want to keep, only retrieving to your computer the messages you want. Thus you needn't clutter up your computer with unnecessary mail, however, you might need to be online for some time sifting through the mail

➤ doing all mail retrieval in a single scheduled operation means you need only be online for just the time it takes to do the retrieval. What's more, CompuServe 2000 will do this for you automatically — you needn't even be there at the time. On the other hand, every mail message you receive must be retrieved — whether you want to store it or not.

These two methods require slightly different techniques at your computer.

Before we reach the point of sending and receiving mail, however, we have to make sure that the mail interface you see on your computer is the same as that shown in this book. Follow the steps overleaf to do that.

Mail preferences

CompuServe 2000's mail preferences are used to set the way that CompuServe 2000 handles outgoing (messages you send to others) and incoming (messages you receive from others) mail.

Basically, as we are going to start using CompuServe 2000 as an online mail system, we will (initially, at least) be following the mail procedures while connected to CompuServe. However, we need to make sure that any messages you send or receive are downloaded to your computer so they are not lost.

Follow the steps here to make sure this will happen.

Basic steps:

1 Choose **Mail Centre↪ Mail Preferences** to call up the **Mail Preferences** dialog box (you don't need to be online to do this)

2 Check the **Save in the Personal Filing Cabinet all mail sent**, and **Save in the Personal Filing Cabinet all mail read** checkboxes

3 Check or uncheck other controls to suit

4 Click **OK**

Tip:

You need to set your mail preferences so that what you see on screen is the same as (or, at least, similar to) the screen shots shown in this section. Setting the mail preferences this way will prevent any mail you send or receive being lost, as it ensures that all mail is saved on your computer. You can choose to delete mail messages later if you want, on a manual basis.

Later on, when we have used this online method for a while we will change to the scheduling method to see the difference. Scheduling mail automatically saves received mail on your computer, by default

③

Set options

This control sets CompuServe 2000 to tell you when a mail message has been successfully sent

Call up the **Mail Preferences** dialog box, by choosing **Mail Centre↦Mail Preferences**

①

This control automatically closes a mail message once it has been sent

This control sets CompuServe 2000 to tell you that a mail message will be sent later

Check these two checkboxes **②**

Check this checkbox to make CompuServe 2000 check the spelling of every mail message automatically before sending them

Mail headers are text information included along with a mail message that describe a message's progress over CompuServe and the Internet

Other people's email addresses can be displayed within mail messages as Internet-style hyperlinks (which use the mailt: e-mail protocol — see page 62). Leave unchecked for now

With this checkbox checked, any viewed mail messages you delete are replaced on screen by the next message

Mail Preferences

☑ **Confirm mail after it has been sent**
☑ **Close mail after it has been sent**
☑ **Confirm when mail is to be sent later**
☑ **Save in the Personal Filing Cabinet all mail sent**
☑ **Save in the Personal Filing Cabinet all mail read**
☐ **Perform a spell check before sending mail**
☑ **Use white mail headers**
☐ **Show addresses as hyperlinks**
☐ **Display next message when current message is deleted**

◉ **Use CompuServe style quoting:**   ○ **Use Internet style quoting:**

<<This is an example of CompuServe style quoting>>

>This is an example
>of internet style quoting

Keep my old mail online [3] days after I read it

[OK]   [Cancel]

④ Click

Mail messages you read while online are kept for a time on the CompuServe network before they are automatically deleted. Leave the time as 3 days (the default) for now

When you reply to a mail message, you can opt to quote some of the message you received in your message. There are various methods of doing this. CompuServe 2000 lets you do it in two ways. Select the Use CompuServe style quoting radio box for the moment. We'll look at the Internet style quoting method later (see Tip on page 101)

Writing and sending mail

Writing CompuServe mail is kids' stuff. Even my seven year old does it! All you need is the person's mail address.

Use my address and send me a message — I can't promise you a personalised reply (in fact, the only thing I *will* try to send is an automated — and very *im*personal — response, for which I apologise in advance) but at least you'll have sent a mail message of your very own.

If you take up this offer, I'd be grateful if you could include some general information along with your mail message to me — that way I can use your comments as research, and make following editions of this book more helpful to other new CompuServe 2000 users.

Enter the following information for me into this mail message:

1 how useful you've found this book overall

2 which areas are particularly helpful

3 which areas could be improved (along with — non-frivolous, please — suggestions how I can improve them)

1 Log onto CompuServe

2 Click the **Create Mail** button on the **Main Menu** toolbar

3 In the **Create Mail** window, type my mail address — `brindley` — in the **Send to** field

4 Enter the message subject `About your book` in the **Subject** field

5 Enter the details of the message into the main message field

6 Click the **Send Now** button to send the message to me

7 If you've setup your mail preferences as on the previous pages (if not, why not? Eh?) you'll now see the **Your mail has been sent** dialog box. Click **OK**

Take note:

It's important you enter the subject of the message exactly as in step 4 as I'll be using an automatic e-mail tool to generate a response whenever I receive a mail with the subject line `About your book` via my CompuServe 2000 account

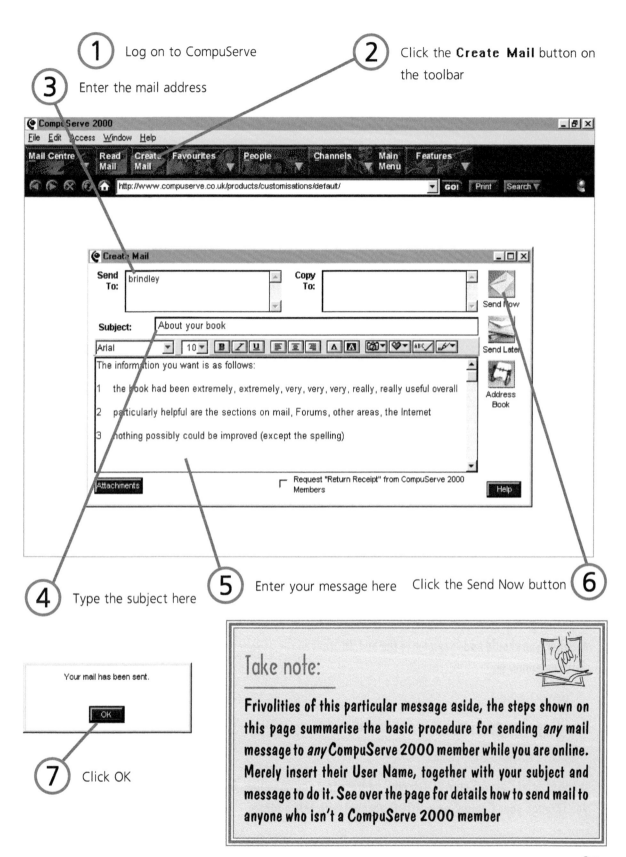

(1) Log on to CompuServe

(2) Click the **Create Mail** button on the toolbar

(3) Enter the mail address

(4) Type the subject here

(5) Enter your message here

(6) Click the Send Now button

(7) Click OK

Your mail has been sent.

OK

Take note:

Frivolities of this particular message aside, the steps shown on this page summarise the basic procedure for sending *any* mail message to *any* CompuServe 2000 member while you are online. Merely insert their User Name, together with your subject and message to do it. See over the page for details how to send mail to anyone who isn't a CompuServe 2000 member

Mail to a non-member

While, as we've seen, sending mail to a member of CompuServe 2000 is as easy as entering the person's CompuServe 2000 User Name, sending mail to someone who *isn't* a member of CompuServe 2000 is just a little more tricky.

Basically, all you need to remember is that where CompuServe 2000 ends, the Internet starts — in other words, if the person isn't a CompuServe 2000 member, CompuServe 2000 sends the mail message via the Internet.

You just have to remind CompuServe 2000 that you want to send a message via the Internet, that's all. To do this, you only need type in the person's Internet e-mail address, which will have a standard URL form something like:

```
email_account@domain_name.co.uk
```

1 Follow steps 1 and 2 on the previous page

2 Enter the address to send the message to, according to the standard Internet e-mail addressing format

3 Enter the subject and message in the usual way

4 Send the mail message in the usual way

Tip:

If you're giving your CompuServe 2000 mail address to someone who isn't a CompuServe 2000 member, you should add @cs.com to the end. In other words, if your mail address to another CompuServe 2000 member is:

```
yourname
```

you always have to remember to add the extra @cs.com to the end, which means that:

```
yourname@cs.com
```

is the official CompuServe 2000 mail address to a non-member. Anyone on the Internet can now reach you through your CompuServe 2000 account with this address

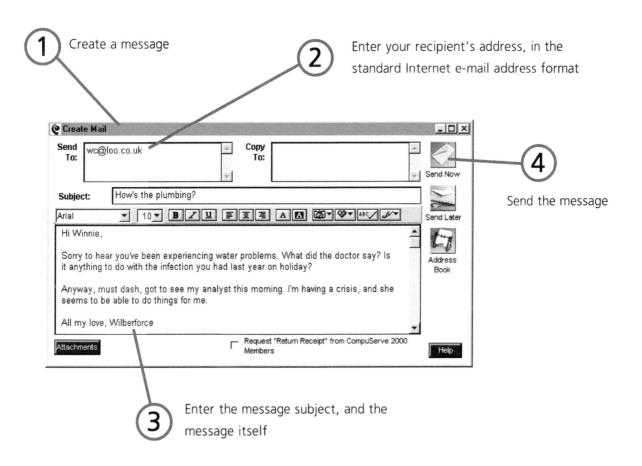

1 Create a message

2 Enter your recipient's address, in the standard Internet e-mail address format

4 Send the message

3 Enter the message subject, and the message itself

Take note:

Entering a person's e-mail address according to the method:

```
email_account@domain_name.co.uk
```

merely instructs CompuServe 2000 to forward the mail message out of CompuServe 2000 onto the Internet. In all but a handful of cases this is all that's required to reach anyone worldwide. However, if you know a person's e-mail address to be on a network other than CompuServe 2000 or the Internet, then CompuServe 2000 may still be able to send it directly — with the Internet as the intermediary medium.

Check with your recipient first if you want, or just fire away and send the message anyway. If the address doesn't exist, you'll receive a bounced message telling you so

Mail bags

CompuServe 2000 has some extremely nice tricks up its sleeve when it comes to mail. Here we show some of the goodies that grace the CompuServe 2000 mail interface.

① Click Create Mail

Basic steps:

1 Create a mail message, by clicking the **Create Mail** button of the toolbar

2 Write a mail message

Italic

Typesize selection

Underline

Text colour

Align right

Background colour   Insert picture

Insert a favourite place

Font selection

Bold

Align left

Centre

Spell check

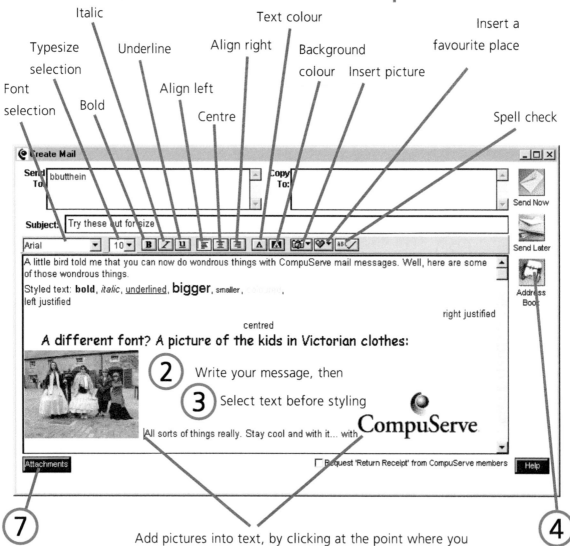

② Write your message, then

③ Select text before styling

⑦

Add an attachment (see Note right, and page 104)

Add pictures into text, by clicking at the point where you want the picture, then clicking the Add Picture button on the mail toolbar — in the following dialog box, locate the file

④

Click to access the Address Book (see page 106)

3 Select words, phrases, sentences and so on, then click a button on the mail toolbar to change text styling

4 Use the **Address Book** to help you address the message — see Tip below

5 Select a person to address the message to

6 Click the **Send To** button

7 Click the **Attachments** button to attach a file to the message to send to your recipient

Take note:

In CompuServe 2000, files you attach are called *attachments*. In some mail programs, files are known as *enclosures* and so the process is called *enclosing*. See pages 104–105, and 140–141 for further important information about file attachment

Take note:

Styled text — bold, italic, fonts and so on — along with on-page graphics, are only available for mail to other CompuServe 2000 users. If you send such a mail message to outside users they may not see the results as you create them. They may just get a plain text (that is, with no styling) message which informs them that graphics are missing

⑤ Select a Name & Address in the Address Book list

Click **Send To**

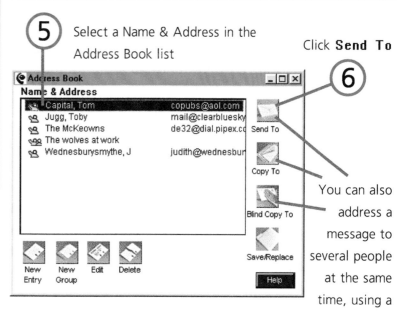

⑥

You can also address a message to several people at the same time, using a combination of these buttons — see pages 102–103 on *multiple recipients*

Tip:

The Address Book is a great way to store names and addresses of all the people you might send a mail message to — see pages 106–107 on setting up your Address Book

Receiving mail

Basic steps:

To receive mail within CompuServe, you first have to be online. Note though that new mail is stored for you by CompuServe, in your Online Mailbox, when you're *not* online — so you won't lose it. Unread mail is stored for 27 days in your Online Mailbox, adequately covering most long holidays or absences.

The way your mail preferences are set up greatly affects the way you can handle received mail messages. Make sure your preferences are setup as shown already (on pages 78–79). If they are, then any mail you read is saved for you (that is, it is a copy is downloaded from your Online Mailbox automatically to your computer). It is stored in your Personal Filing Cabinet (see pages 91–93), where you can read it again, keep it handy, file it in an archive, or delete it.

On the other hand, any mail in your Online Mailbox that you read will be deleted automatically by CompuServe, a set period (three days, by default) after you first read it. So, if your CompuServe 2000 preferences aren't as suggested, you may lose mail messages you've read online if you're not careful.

1   Logon to CompuServe

2   If the **Read Mail** button is highlighted in yellow text, click it

3   Click to select any message in your Online Mailbox

4   Click the **Read** button to open the message (or double-click the message at step 3)

contd...

Tip:

When you logon to CompuServe at any time, keep an eye on the Read Mail button on the toolbar.

If it says Read Mail in yellow, that means you've got mail messages waiting. If your computer has sound ability, you will get a voice message telling you there are messages waiting, too

---

Take note:

This procedure of logging on, reading mail, then logging off, while fairly easy to understand, is not a particularly efficient way of managing your mail. It is, however, a good method of learning what CompuServe mail is all about — which is why I suggest you use it (for the time being, at least).

A much better method is scheduling — covered on pages 94–97

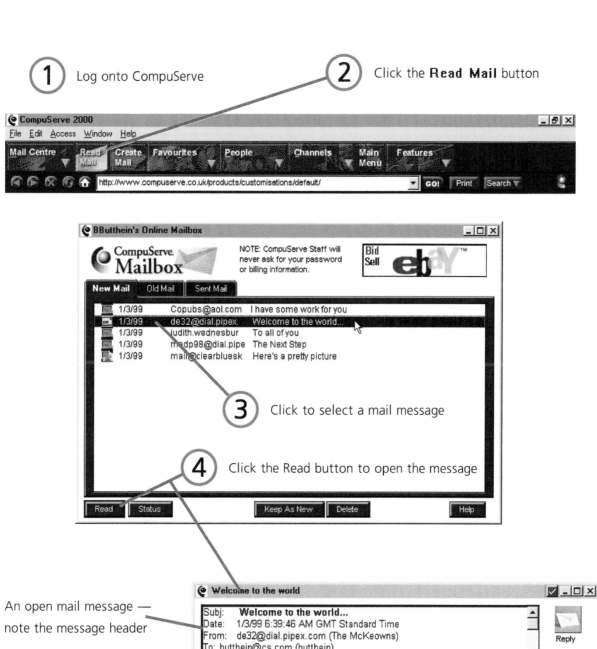

① Log onto CompuServe

② Click the **Read Mail** button

③ Click to select a mail message

④ Click the Read button to open the message

An open mail message —
note the message header

You've got...
...mail
Come and get it!

Receiving mail (contd)

Tip:

Remember that once you've opened a mail message while online, your mail preferences are set so that the message is downloaded to your computer and stored in your **Personal Filing Cabinet**, where you can read it – at your leisure – at any time.

In other words, you don't need to spend online time (which is costing you a phone call) reading messages in detail

5 Scroll down the message to view it all, if you want

6 Close the message

7 Repeat steps 3–6 to open other messages, or disconnect from CompuServe by choosing **Access→Disconnect** or typing `Ctrl`+`D`

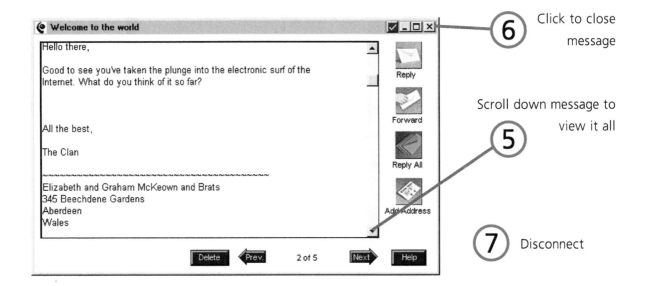

⑥ Click to close message

⑤ Scroll down message to view it all

⑦ Disconnect

Tip:

If you have a number of mail messages in your Online Mailbox, you don't have to spend time opening then closing each one individually. The mail message window has buttons that allow you to step through messages. Just open the first mail message, then click the Next button repeatedly, until you reach the last message. All messages will then have been opened and downloaded to your computer

Basic steps:

1 Open your **Personal Filing Cabinet** by choosing **Mail Centre⌐Personal Filing Cabinet**, or type `Ctrl` + `F`

2 Click a mail message you want to read in the **Incoming/Saved Mail** folder of the **Personal Filing Cabinet**

3 Click the **Open** button to read the message

contd...

Reading mail

Once you have retrieved any messages from your Online Mailbox and disconnected from the CompuServe network, you are ready to read the messages, reply to them, delete them or store them as you want.

All received mail messages, by default are placed in the **Incoming/Saved Mail** folder of your Personal Filing Cabinet.

(**1**) Choose **Mail Centre⌐Personal Filing Cabinet**

(**2**) Select the mail message you want to read, by clicking it

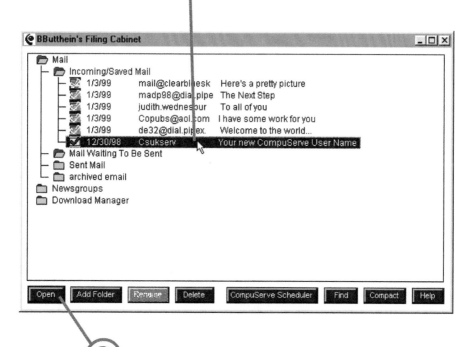

(**3**) Click **Open** to read the mail message

89

Reading mail (contd)

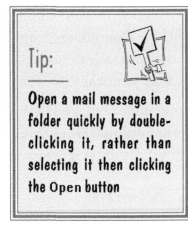

Tip:

Open a mail message in a folder quickly by double-clicking it, rather than selecting it then clicking the Open button

4 The message is seen in its own window — with top header information saying when it was sent, and where it came from

5 Scroll down the message

6 To delete the message (that is, if you don't want to keep it), click **Delete**

7 Alternatively, (if you *do* want to keep the message), click the message's Close Box to close the message

Or:

8 Step through the other mail messages in the folder by clicking the **Prev** or **Next** buttons

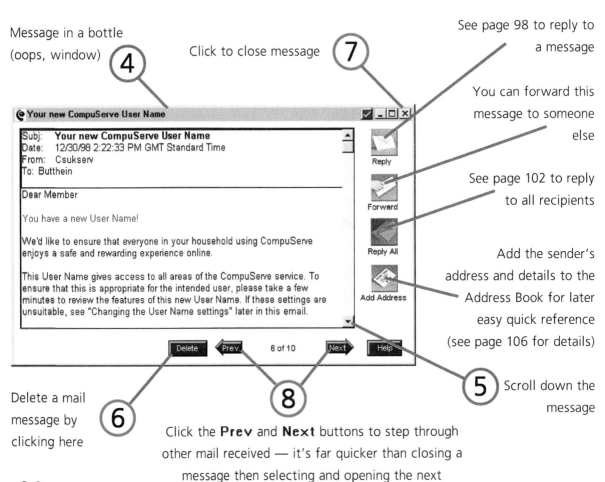

Message in a bottle (oops, window) ④

Click to close message ⑦

See page 98 to reply to a message

You can forward this message to someone else

See page 102 to reply to all recipients

Add the sender's address and details to the Address Book for later easy quick reference (see page 106 for details)

⑤ Scroll down the message

Delete a mail message by clicking here ⑥

⑧

Click the **Prev** and **Next** buttons to step through other mail received — it's far quicker than closing a message then selecting and opening the next

Personal Filing Cabinet

Basic steps:

1 Select a folder in the **Personal Filing Cabinet**

2 Click the **Open** button to to open the folder and display its contents in a hierarchy (or just double-click the folder at step 1)

3 Repeat steps 1 & 2 for all other folders and sub-folders

contd...

We've briefly used it, but now we're going to take a closer look at it.

Your **Personal Filing Cabinet** (PFC) is an area within the CompuServe 2000 client on your computer, where you are able to store things. Files you download, incoming and outgoing mail messages, and so on, are all stored here.

The **Personal Filing Cabinet** operates in much the same way that Windows Explorer does

Repeat steps 1 & 2 for all other folders and sub-folders

③

Click **Open** ②

Click a folder to select it

①

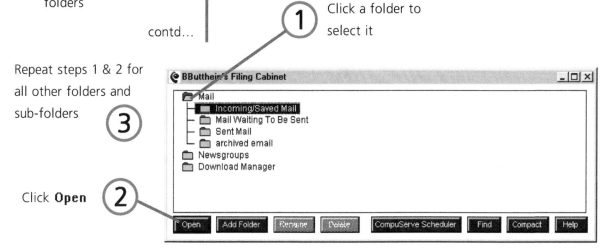

Take note:

As your Personal Filing Cabinet contains items you have downloaded or created at your own computer, it follows that it is only accessible from your computer — you can't access it if you are logged on as a Guest on the CompuServe 2000 client on someone else's computer.

Further, you can't access your Personal Filing Cabinet if you are logged on to CompuServe at your own computer, but using another User Name — a useful security feature

PFC (contd)

As you open folders and sub-folders within the **Personal Filing Cabinet**, individual items become visible.

These individual items can be moved, deleted, opened, and generally manipulated in several ways.

Icon changes to show the file being dragged, as you drop it onto another folder's icon — here the mail message **About your book** is about to be dropped into the **archived email** folder

Mail messages already read have a ticked icon

Empty, open folders are represented by an open folder icon, with no files in the hierarchy

Basic steps (contd):

4   You can select any item within the **Personal Filing Cabinet** by clicking it

5   Open any selected item by clicking the **Open** button (or just double-click the item at step 4)

6   You can manipulate items by dragging and dropping them into other folders

Click an item to select it

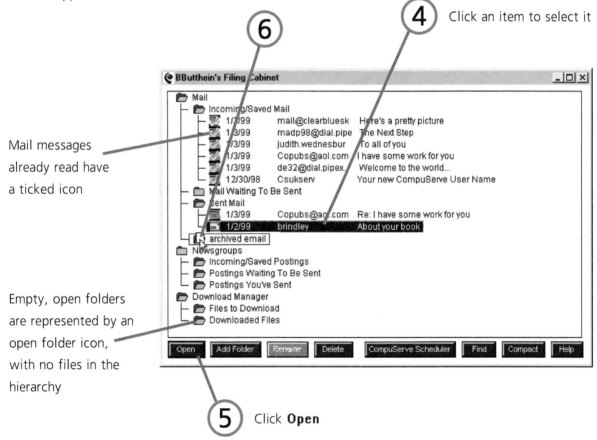

Click **Open**

7 Create new folders (or sub-folders) by clicking where you want the folder to be, then;

8 Click the **Add Folder** button

9 In the **New Folder** dialog box, enter the name of the new folder you want

10 Click **OK** to create the new folder

Tip:

While manipulating items within the Personal Filing Cabinet, you can use some shortcuts:

▷ select multiple non-contiguous items by `Ctrl`+clicking them
▷ select a batch of items by `Shift`+clicking the first and the last in the batch
▷ deselect items from a selection, by `Ctrl`+clicking items you don't want

⑦ Click where you want a new folder to be — in this case, clicking the **Mail** folder allows a new sub-folder to be created within it

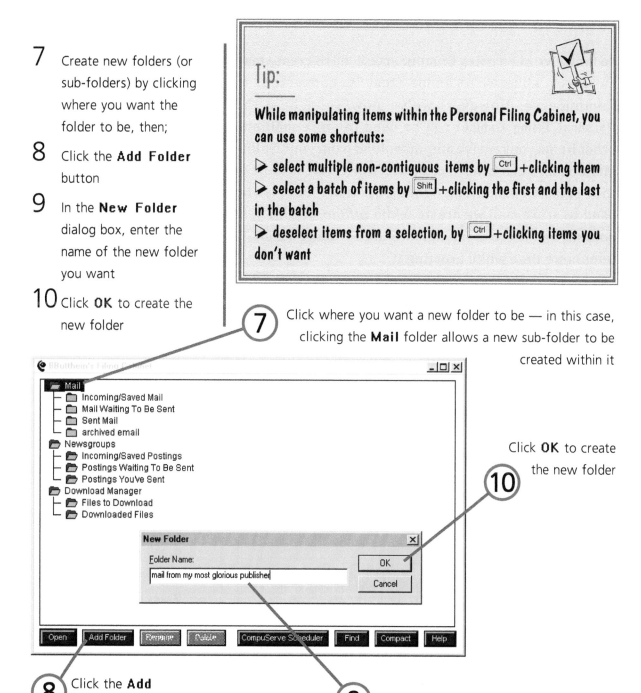

Click **OK** to create the new folder ⑩

⑧ Click the **Add Folder** button

⑨

The **New Folder** dialog box allows us to name the folder. Fortunately, the contents of the **Personal Filing Cabinet** are private so we call the new folder exactly what we... err, want, knowing that nobody else will see it (just as well, eh?)

93

Sending mail later

So far we've been using CompuServe 2000 to create mail messages while we're online (that is, connected) to CompuServe. However, we've now seen how the **Personal Filing Cabinet** can be used to store mail and other items you receive and download from your Online Mailbox and elsewhere on the network. The benefit of the **Personal Filing Cabinet**, though, is that it can also be used to store mail we create while *offline* — which, of course, has the benefit that we aren't using valuable telephone time while creating it.

The idea is that mail messages are stored in the **Personal Filing Cabinet** after creating the messages, until the next time we log onto CompuServe.

The procedure to do the job — called scheduling — is worth getting to grips with, as it can save loads of time — and, hence, money — in the long run. It simply is the fastest way of sending and receiving all your mail.

Basic steps:

1 While offline, click the **Create Mail** button on the toolbar

2 Enter a mail address in the **Send To** field

3 Enter a message subject

4 Type in your message

5 Click the **Send Later** button

6 If you have further messages to create, click the **OK** button, then repeat steps 1–5 for more new messages

7 When you have finished creating messages, and want to send them, click the **CompuServe Scheduler** button

8 In the **CompuServe Scheduler Preferences** window, click the **Select Names** button

                    contd...

Take note:

You *can* create, read, and reply to mail all while you are online, as we have been doing so far. But the best use of CompuServe is made by doing these functions offline — the way we do it on these and the following pages — this can save your online charges and lower your telephone bill.

In other words, you only need to logon to receive and send your mail. All reading and writing of mail can (and, from now on, *should*) be carried out offline

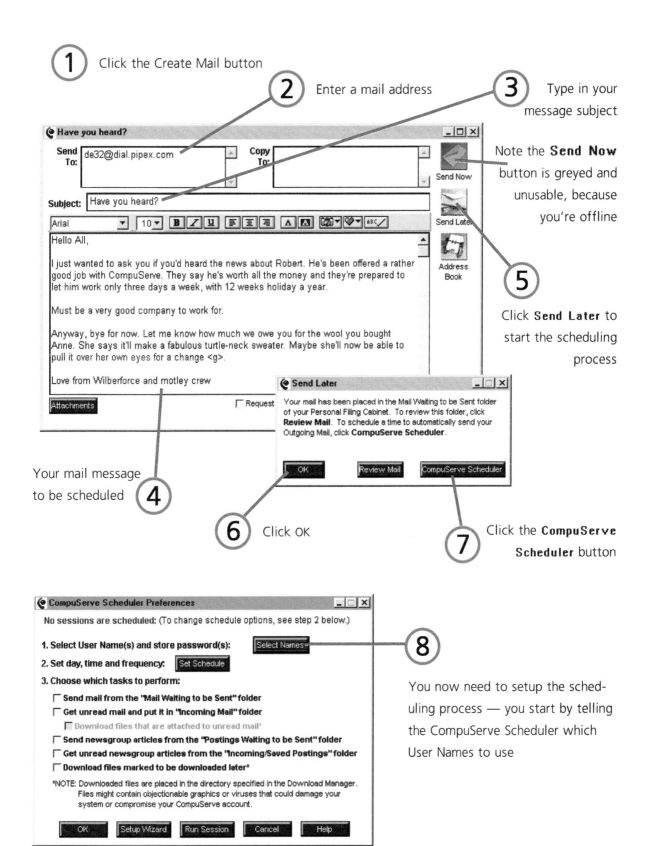

(1) Click the Create Mail button

(2) Enter a mail address

(3) Type in your message subject

Note the **Send Now** button is greyed and unusable, because you're offline

(5) Click **Send Later** to start the scheduling process

Your mail message to be scheduled (4)

(6) Click OK

(7) Click the **CompuServe Scheduler** button

(8) You now need to setup the scheduling process — you start by telling the CompuServe Scheduler which User Names to use

Have you heard?

Send To: de32@dial.pipex.com
Copy To:
Send Now
Send Later
Address Book

Subject: Have you heard?

Arial | 10 | **B** *I* U | ≡ ≡ ≡ | A A | | ABC

Hello All,

I just wanted to ask you if you'd heard the news about Robert. He's been offered a rather good job with CompuServe. They say he's worth all the money and they're prepared to let him work only three days a week, with 12 weeks holiday a year.

Must be a very good company to work for.

Anyway, bye for now. Let me know how much we owe you for the wool you bought Anne. She says it'll make a fabulous turtle-neck sweater. Maybe she'll now be able to pull it over her own eyes for a change <g>.

Love from Wilberforce and motley crew

Attachments | ☐ Request

Send Later

Your mail has been placed in the Mail Waiting to be Sent folder of your Personal Filing Cabinet. To review this folder, click **Review Mail**. To schedule a time to automatically send your Outgoing Mail, click **CompuServe Scheduler**.

OK | Review Mail | CompuServe Scheduler

CompuServe Scheduler Preferences

No sessions are scheduled: (To change schedule options, see step 2 below.)

1. Select User Name(s) and store password(s): Select Names

2. Set day, time and frequency: Set Schedule

3. Choose which tasks to perform:

☐ Send mail from the "Mail Waiting to be Sent" folder
☐ Get unread mail and put it in "Incoming Mail" folder
  ☐ Download files that are attached to unread mail*
☐ Send newsgroup articles from the "Postings Waiting to be Sent" folder
☐ Get unread newsgroup articles from the "Incoming/Saved Postings" folder
☐ Download files marked to be downloaded later*

*NOTE: Downloaded files are placed in the directory specified in the Download Manager. Files might contain objectionable graphics or viruses that could damage your system or compromise your CompuServe account.

OK | Setup Wizard | Run Session | Cancel | Help

95

Sending mail later (contd)

Now you're about to see some of the real power of scheduling within CompuServe 2000. It's the fact that all mail sending and receiving is done at top speed.

9 Check the checkbox of the User Name you wish to use in the schedule (generally the one you always use) and enter the password in the **Password** field

Select User Names

User Name	Password
☑ BButthein	*****
☐ Closely	
☐ Mail2send	

Note: Storing your passwords does not change them. To change your passwords, please GO PASSWORD when you're online.

[OK] [Cancel]

10 Click **OK**

We're going to schedule a session that sends all the mail you have created while offline, and stored within your **Personal Filing Cabinet**, as well as download *to* your **Personal Filing Cabinet** any mail that you have received that's waiting in your Online Mailbox for you to read

9 In the **Select User Names** dialog box, check the box associated with the User Name you want to use, and enter the password associated with it (see pages 130–132 for a description of names and passwords)

10 Click **OK**

11 Back in the **CompuServe Scheduler Preferences** window, check the two controls shown

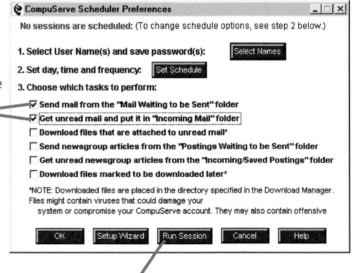

CompuServe Scheduler Preferences

No sessions are scheduled: (To change schedule options, see step 2 below.)

1. Select User Name(s) and save password(s): [Select Names]
2. Set day, time and frequency: [Set Schedule]
3. Choose which tasks to perform:

☑ **Send mail from the "Mail Waiting to be Sent" folder**
☑ **Get unread mail and put it in "Incoming Mail" folder**
☐ Download files that are attached to unread mail*
☐ Send newsgroup articles from the "Postings Waiting to be Sent" folder
☐ Get unread newsgroup articles from the "Incoming/Saved Postings" folder
☐ Download files marked to be downloaded later*

*NOTE: Downloaded files are placed in the directory specified in the Download Manager. Files might contain viruses that could damage your system or compromise your CompuServe account. They may also contain offensive

[OK] [Setup Wizard] [Run Session] [Cancel] [Help]

12 Click Run Session

12 Click the **Run Session** button

13 In the resultant **Run CompuServe Scheduler Session Now** dialog box, click **Begin**

Run CompuServe Scheduler Session Now

Click **Begin** to immediately run a CompuServe Scheduler session for the Member Name you are using now. The tasks you have chosen will occur. If you want to review or change the tasks you have chosen, click **Review Tasks** instead.

NOTE: Files might contain objectionable graphics or viruses that could damage your system or compromise your CompuServe account. If your New Mail list contains e-mail with attached files, make sure you know who sent you the mail before you start this CompuServe Scheduler session. To retrieve unread mail without downloading attached files, click the **Review Tasks** button and verify the Download Files option is not checked.

☐ **Stay connected when finished**

[Begin]   [Review Tasks]   [Cancel]

Phew – done it!

13 At long last — here we are — click this button to perform the schedule

Yes, you've finally got there. After step 13, CompuServe 2000 now goes away and performs the schedule. It logs your computer onto CompuServe, carries out all mail transfer (sending mail you've created, and downloading any mail received in your Online Mailbox), then logs itself back off again — all automatically, and all extremely quickly.

As it does all this, progress is displayed in the Status window within the CompuServe 2000 client.

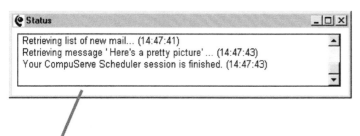

Status

Retrieving list of new mail... (14:47:41)
Retrieving message 'Here's a pretty picture'... (14:47:43)
Your CompuServe Scheduler session is finished. (14:47:43)

The Status window of CompuServe 2000 shows the scheduled tasks as they occur — from this one you can see that only a few seconds occur between the process starting and it stopping. Mail scheduling occurs far faster than you can possibly hope to achieve manually

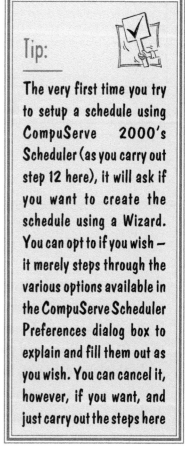

Tip:

The very first time you try to setup a schedule using CompuServe 2000's Scheduler (as you carry out step 12 here), it will ask if you want to create the schedule using a Wizard. You can opt to if you wish — it merely steps through the various options available in the CompuServe Scheduler Preferences dialog box to explain and fill them out as you wish. You can cancel it, however, if you want, and just carry out the steps here

Replying to mail

Unlike *snailmail*, where you have to write a new envelope to reply to a received letter, CompuServe mail messages are much easier to reply to.

In CompuServe mail you receive, there's a **Reply** button for the very job.

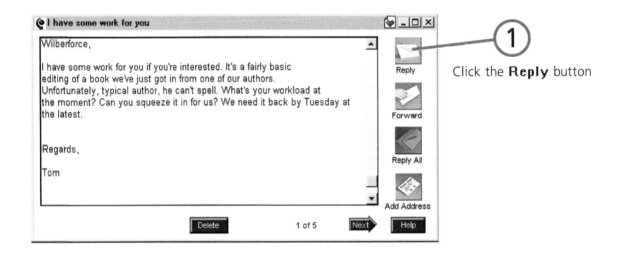

Click the **Reply** button

<table>
<tr><td>

Take note:

You can reply to mail messages while you are either online – reading mail messages in your Online Mailbox – or offline, reading retrieved messages stored in you Personal Filing Cabinet (see pages 91–93). However, if you are working offline then you will not be able to send the reply immediately. Instead, you will either have to go online and manually send them, or set up a schedule to do the job for you (see pages 94–97)

</td><td>

Take note:

While CompuServe mail is incredibly fast at sending messages anywhere around the world, if you only logon once every other Thursday its speed becomes somewhat irrelevant

</td></tr>
</table>

3 Click **Send Later** (or **Send** if you are online and want to send the reply immediately). There's no need to enter the recipient's name, mail address, or the message subject — they are all added automatically by CompuServe 2000

Tip:

Remember that CompuServe mail is like a conversation spread out over a period of time. While it can take literally minutes to be delivered anywhere in the world, often it can be hours, or even days, before the recipient will read and reply to a received message.

Because of this, in anything other than the simplest of cases, it's always best to refer to previous parts of the mail discussion to remind the recipient. Over the page you'll find a technique (called *reply-quoting*) which gives you this ability, without having to copy out by hand the text you want to quote

3 Click **Send Later**, or **Send Now**

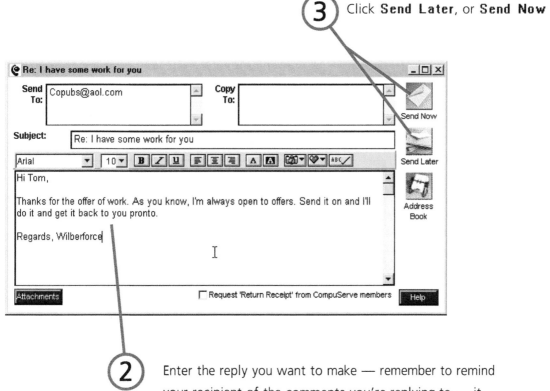

2 Enter the reply you want to make — remember to remind your recipient of the comments you're replying to — it may be days before the recipient reads it (see Tip above)

Reply-quoting mail

You can quote parts of a mail message you have received in your reply. This is called *reply-quoting*. It's useful if you only need to refer to one or two parts of the original message, and is a good reminder of what has been referred to in past messages. For this reason, reply-quoted text can pass on through several replies between recipients.

It's usual to insert some character which shows that text is reply-quoted (so that the quote doesn't get mixed up with new text), and the one used almost universally by default is the *greater than* symbol character: >. In CompuServe mail, the *less than* character: < traditionally ends reply-quoted text.

1 In an open mail message you have received, select the text you want to reply-quote

2 Click the **Reply** button. This creates a **Reply** message window, in which the reply-quoted text is visible

3 In the **Reply** message window, enter your reply

4 **Send Now** or **Send Later**, as usual

Take note:

Note that CompuServe's use of the greater than and less than symbols is different to the standard Internet method of indicating reply-quoted text, in which the greater than symbol precedes every line (in other words, a line without the greater than symbol is not reply-quoted!)

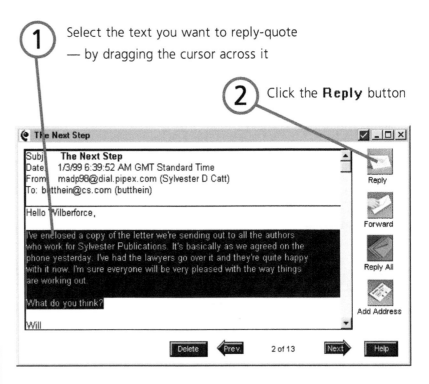

Select the text you want to reply-quote
— by dragging the cursor across it

Click the **Reply** button

Tip:

If you use CompuServe 2000's mail facility regularly to send and receive e-mail to and from non-CompuServe 2000 users, you may find it best to opt to use the standard Internet-style reply-quoting method. Select the Use Internet style quoting radio button of the Mail Preferences dialog box for this — see page 78

③

The text you highlighted in your received mail message becomes the reply-quoted text in your newly-created outgoing mail message. Simply type in your reply to the message where you want

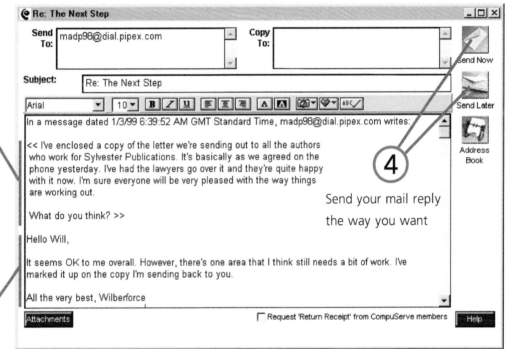

Send your mail reply the way you want

④

Tip:

Using Internet-style reply-quoting, it's easy to split reply-quoted text to insert your responses at several points — rather than just at the end — that's the Internet-style method's beauty. You *can* break reply-quoted text to insert your response when you're using the traditional CompuServe-style reply-quoting, but remember to add corresponding less than and greater than symbols to show where the splits occur

Reply to all

Occasionally, you might receive a mail message that has been sent to several people. You can choose to reply to only the author of the original message in the same way we've considered earlier. However, you can send your reply to all recipients of the mail message. Recipients are listed in the message header — although see the note below.

Basic steps:

1 In the mail message window, click the **Reply All** button

2 In the **Reply** window type your reply

3 Click **Send** or **Send Later**

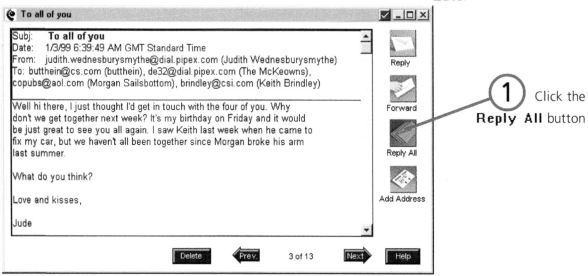

① Click the **Reply All** button

Take note:

Any message can be sent to more than one recipient. There are, actually, three types of recipient:

▷ **To – main recipients. All other recipients can see who main recipients are**

▷ **cc – (carbon copy) – not a main recipient, but who may be interested or involved in the message. All other recipients can see who carbon copy recipients are**

▷ **bcc – (blind carbon copy) – no other recipients (even another blind carbon copy recipient) can see whether there are blind carbon copy recipients. Because of this, you can use blind carbon copying when you want to send copies of messages confidentially**

Send the message in the usual way ③

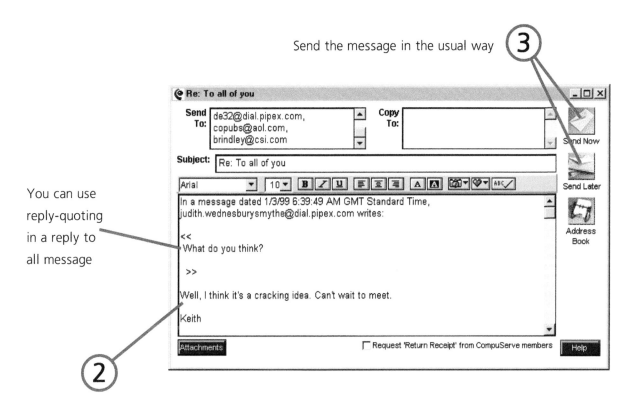

You can use
reply-quoting
in a reply to
all message

②

The message itself

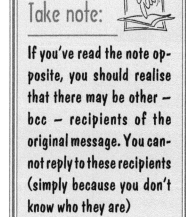

Take note:

If you've read the note opposite, you should realise that there may be other — bcc — recipients of the original message. You cannot reply to these recipients (simply because you don't know who they are)

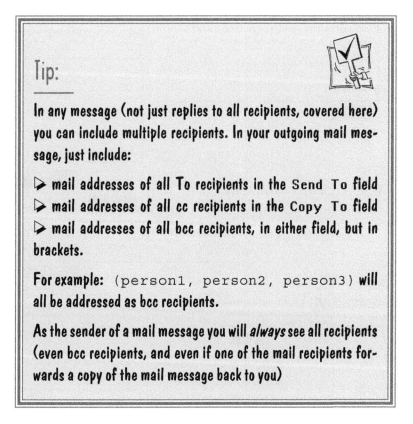

Tip:

In any message (not just replies to all recipients, covered here) you can include multiple recipients. In your outgoing mail message, just include:

▷ mail addresses of all To recipients in the Send To field
▷ mail addresses of all cc recipients in the Copy To field
▷ mail addresses of all bcc recipients, in either field, but in brackets.

For example: (person1, person2, person3) will all be addressed as bcc recipients.

As the sender of a mail message you will *always* see all recipients (even bcc recipients, and even if one of the mail recipients forwards a copy of the mail message back to you)

Attaching files

One of the beauties about CompuServe mail is that computer files can be sent along with a mail message. This means that a word processed document, for example, fully formatted with graphic images and styles can be sent electronically from user to user to view, print out, and work with. It also means that graphic files, spreadsheets, databases, even complete applications can be attached.

Basic steps:

1 In a **Create Mail** window, enter the name and address of your recipient, and message in the usual way

2 Click the **Attach File** button

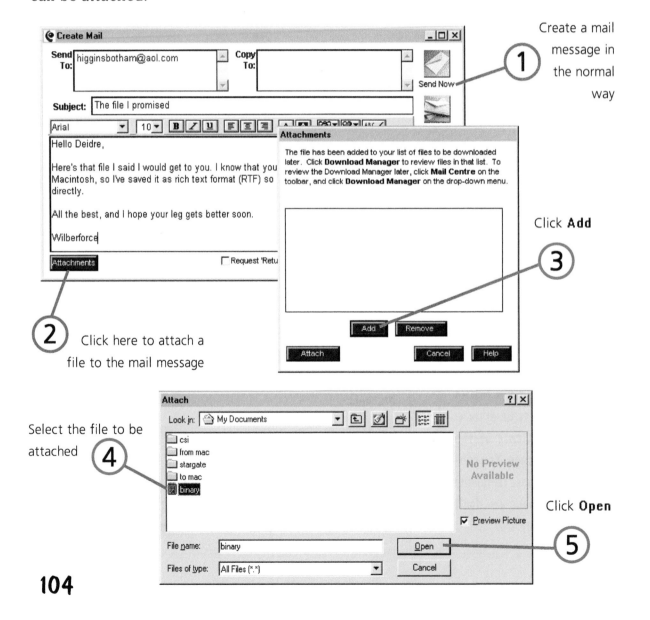

Create a mail message in the normal way ①

Click here to attach a file to the mail message ②

Click **Add** ③

Select the file to be attached ④

Click **Open** ⑤

3 In the resultant **Attachments** dialog box, click the **Add** button

4 In the Attach dialog box, locate and select the file you want to attach

5 Click **Open**

6 Back in the **Attachments** dialog box, click **Attach**

7 Send the mail message in the usual way

Click the **Attach** button

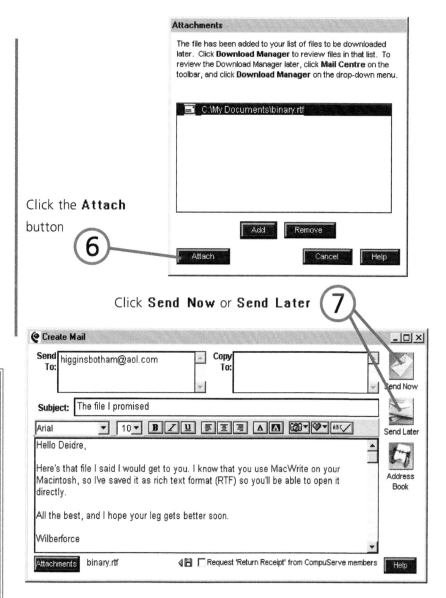

Attachments

The file has been added to your list of files to be downloaded later. Click **Download Manager** to review files in that list. To review the Download Manager later, click **Mail Centre** on the toolbar, and click **Download Manager** on the drop-down menu.

☐ C:\My Documents\binary.rtf

Add   Remove

⑥

Attach   Cancel   Help

Click **Send Now** or **Send Later**   ⑦

Create Mail   _ □ ×

Send To: higginsbotham@aol.com   Copy To: Send Now

Subject: The file I promised   Send Later

Arial   ▼ 10 ▼ **B** *I* U ≡ ≡ ≡ A A ▦▼ ♥▼ ᴬᴮᶜ✓

Hello Deidre,   Address
                                                                                     Book
Here's that file I said I would get to you. I know that you use MacWrite on your
Macintosh, so I've saved it as rich text format (RTF) so you'll be able to open it
directly.

All the best, and I hope your leg gets better soon.

Wilberforce

Attachments binary.rtf   ◄▤ ☐ Request 'Return Receipt' from CompuServe members   Help

Take note:

While this procedure is all that's involved in actually attaching a file to an email message, it's really only the tip of the iceberg. Most important is to make sure that your recipient can use the file.

Pages 140–141 present a strategy to follow when attaching files, which helps to make sure that people you send files to will be able to access them

Tip:

You can attach more than one file to a mail message. Simply click the Add button again, after step 6, and locate further files. Continue steps 3–6 until all the files you want are attached

105

The Address Book

We've already mentioned the Address Book as a convenient way to address mail messages you create. Now we look at how to set up your Address Book. Basically, you add names and addresses to your Address Book in one of two ways:

▷ you can enter the names and addresses manually — the best method if you have someone's mail address given to you, say, on paper or a business card, or by voice over the phone

▷ you can add them with the click of a button — on-the-fly — from within a mail message you receive.

You can also create groups — collections of names and addresses — that you can apply to mail messages you create.

MANUALLY:

1 Choose **Mail Centre ↳ Address Book**, or type `Ctrl` + `B`

2 Click the **New Entry** button

3 In the **New Entry** dialog box, enter the person's name, mail address and any notes you wish to attach

4 Click **OK**

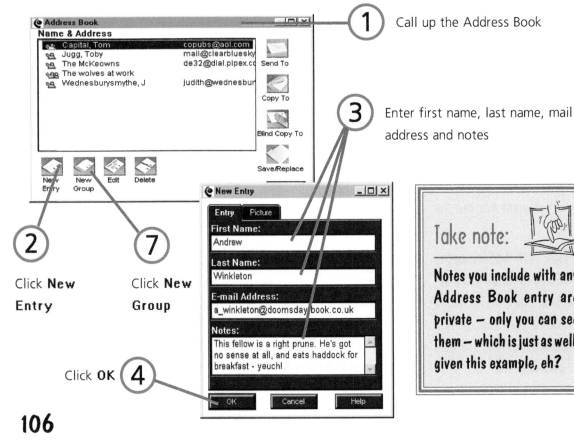

① Call up the Address Book

③ Enter first name, last name, mail address and notes

② Click **New Entry**

⑦ Click **New Group**

Click **OK** ④

Take note:

Notes you include with any Address Book entry are private — only you can see them — which is just as well, given this example, eh?

5 In any mail message you receive, click the **Add Address** button

6 In the resultant **New Entry** dialog box, follow steps 3 & 4

GROUPS:

7 After step 1, click the **New Group** button

8 Enter a name for the group

9 Enter each person's mail address, separated only by a comma

10 Click OK

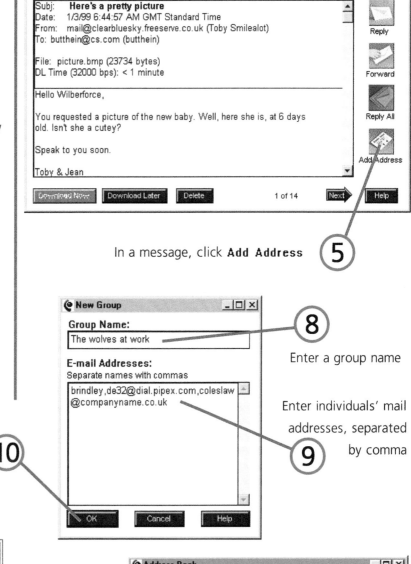

In a message, click **Add Address** (5)

Enter a group name (8)

Enter individuals' mail addresses, separated by comma (9)

Click OK (10)

Tip:

Groups are sometimes called mailing lists in other e-mail programs — set them up and use them when you want to mail several people regularly

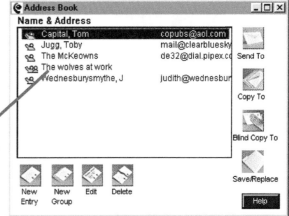

Back in the Address Book, you can tell which entry is a group as it has a different icon

107

Instant Messenger

CompuServe 2000 has a rather neat tool, in the form of CompuServe Instant Messenger. While, officially, it could be classed as just another mailing feature, it is in fact an extremely good communications tool in its own right.

Where e-mail is a method of sending a message via mailboxes, so that people can check their mailboxes at any later time, Instant Messenger allows messages to be passed between people in real-time — in other words… — err, instantly.

Best of all, perhaps, CompuServe 2000's in-built Instant Messenger can be used for messages with people who aren't even CompuServe members. All they need to do is run the free, standalone CompuServe Instant Messenger program to allow this to happen.

Here we look at how to set up a basic Instant Message.

Basic steps:

1. When online, choose **People↳Instant Message**, or type Ctrl+I
2. In the **Send Instant Message** dialog box, type in the User Name of the member you want to communicate with
3. Press the **Available?** button
4. If your chosen member is online, the resultant dialog box tells you. Press **OK** to proceed
5. Type in the message you want to send
6. Press the **Send** button

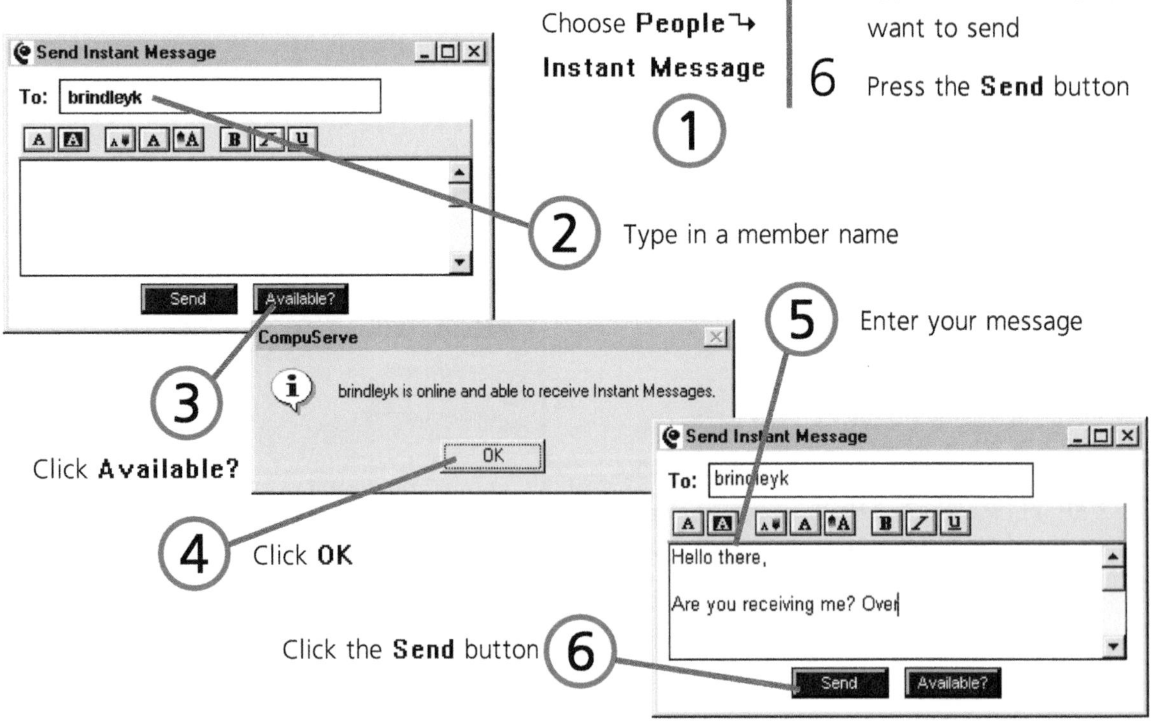

Choose People↳ Instant Message
1
Send Instant Message
To: brindleyk
Send
Available?
2
Type in a member name
3
Click Available?
CompuServe
brindleyk is online and able to receive Instant Messages.
OK
4
Click OK
5
Enter your message
Send Instant Message
To: brindleyk
Hello there,
Are you receiving me? Over
Send
Available?
6
Click the Send button

7 Wait for a response. In the **Instant Message** you receive, click the **Respond** button

8 Type your response into the bottom pane of the **Instant Message** window

9 Click **Send** to send your response

10 Thereafter it's a matter of repeating steps 8–9 until you wish to complete your Instant Message, after which you should click the Instant Message close box

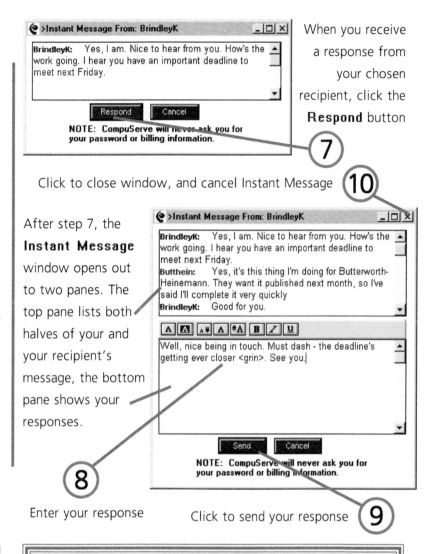

When you receive a response from your chosen recipient, click the **Respond** button

⑦

Click to close window, and cancel Instant Message ⑩

After step 7, the **Instant Message** window opens out to two panes. The top pane lists both halves of your and your recipient's message, the bottom pane shows your responses.

⑧

Enter your response

⑨ Click to send your response

Tip:

Use CompuServe's neat Contact List feature, which can tell you – automatically – whenever your friends, family, or colleagues are online (see pages 142–145)

Tip:

CompuServe has Instant Messenger software available for non-CompuServe members. Tell your friends, family and colleagues to download it from the main CompuServe Instant Messenger Website, at:

http://csim.compuserve.co.uk

to allow them to join in the Instant Messenger fun

Instant Messenger (contd)

Just as you now know to initiate an Instant Message with someone else, so they can do it with you. The first you'll know about it is when the **Instant Message From** window pops up on your CompuServe 2000 desktop while you're online.

1   When an **Instant Message From** window pops up on your desktop, click the **Respond** button

2   In the opened up **Instant Message** window type your response

3   Click the **Send** button, then wait for your recipient's response

4   Continue steps 2 and 3, until your conversation has ended, then click the **Instant Message** window's close box to terminate it

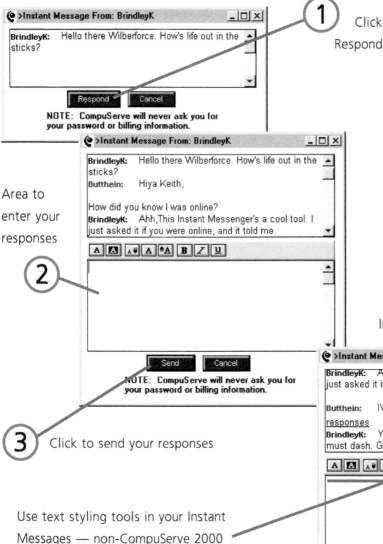

Click Respond

Area to enter your responses

Click to send your responses

Click to end Instant Message

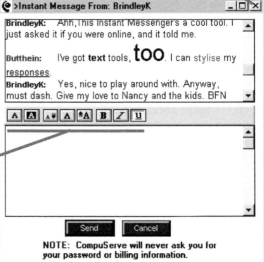

Use text styling tools in your Instant Messages — non-CompuServe 2000 members can also send and receive formatted messages

Basic steps:

1 Choose **Mail Centre⤳ Log Manager**

2 In the resultant **Log Manager** dialog box, click the **Create Log File** button

3 Locate a place to save the log

4 Name the log

5 Click **Save**

6 Check the **Log Instant Messages** checkbox of the **Log Manager** dialog box

7 Continue with your **Instant Message** as before

8 Click the **Close Log File** button when you have finished your conversation

Tip:

Session logs like this can be opened later when offline to read the text at your leisure – this saves online time

Saving Instant Messages

Occasionally, it may be useful to save Instant Messages. You might be discussing something with a client, for example, and wish to keep a record of the Instant Message conversation. You do this by telling CompuServe 2000 to save the Instant Message as a text file — in computerese it's called a *session log*.

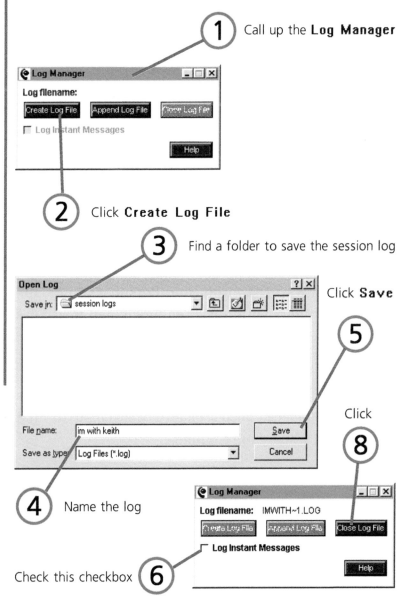

① Call up the **Log Manager**

② Click **Create Log File**

③ Find a folder to save the session log

Click **Save**

⑤

Click

⑧

④ Name the log

Check this checkbox ⑥

Summary for Section 4

Sending mail to CompuServe 2000 memebers is as simple as entering their User Name in the **Send To** field of a new mail message.

Sending mail to non-CompuServe 2000 members is just as easy — just use their Internet-style e-mail address instead.

You can only receive mail while online, but you can create mail while offline.

Use reply-quoting to remind your recipient about something mentioned earlier in your mail 'conversation'.

If you receive a mail message which is circulated to several people you can reply to all people who received the circulated message by clicking the **Reply All** button.

Use CompuServe 2000's multiple recipient facility if you want to send the message to several people.

Your mail is stored within your Personal Filing Cabinet. Creat folders within it, then move mail messages within those folders to keep it neat and tidy.

Make sure your recipient has the ability to handle attached files you send *before* you send them.

Use CompuServe 2000's Instant Messenger to chat with people while you're online.

5 Forums

What are Forums?

Forums are online areas — sorts of electronic clubs — that enable members to exchange information on topics of mutual interest. Just like a club, you join a Forum if it interests you and you use it to suit yourself. You go there if you need specific information, help, or simply just to communicate with other Forum members.

Forums can be accessed within CompuServe 2000 from the **Forum Centre**. All Forums are maintained by people called sysops, who will help members of their Forum and regulate what happens there.

Basic steps:

1 Connect to CompuServe

2 Choose either **People↪Forum Centre**, or **Channels↪ Forum Centre**

3 Locate Forums you want either by clicking a hyperlink, or with the **FIND A FORUM** box

1 Logon to CompuServe

2 Choose **People↪Forum Centre**

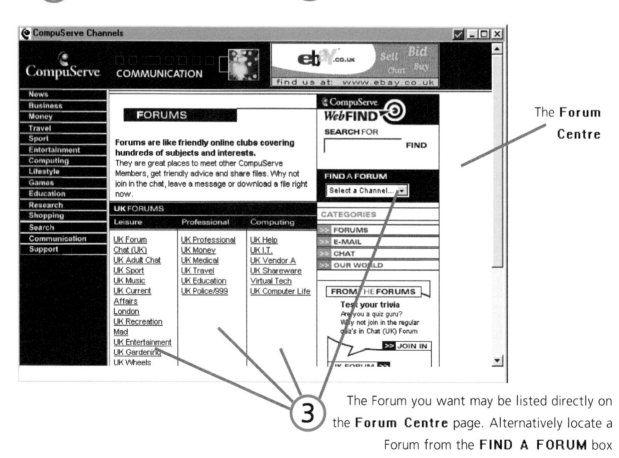

The **Forum Centre**

3 The Forum you want may be listed directly on the **Forum Centre** page. Alternatively locate a Forum from the **FIND A FORUM** box

Take note:

How many Forums are there?

There are quite literally hundreds of Forums on CompuServe. They cover topics as diverse as flower arranging and butterflies, to football and cars. In fact, whatever your interest there's almost certainly a Forum that could interest you. It's impossible to list them all, too — because new Forums are started all the time

Information in a Forum, and the help it can provide depends very much on Forum members. For example, Forum members can exchange messages on message boards, retrieve (download) and contribute (upload) files from and to associated libraries, and meet in electronic conference rooms to chat to other Forum members or listen to an invited speaker.

Message boards

Just like a staff-room corkboard, or a newsagent's door, message boards allow people to place a notice in full sight of other people. Anyone seeing a message can reply to it by also putting a message on a board, and so the chain goes on.

The beauty about a CompuServe Forum message board is that it is open to any member who takes an interest in that particular Forum. In theory, some 5 million or so people could see a message you post. Daunting? Not particularly — the thing about CompuServe Forums is that they are frequented only by members who take an interest in that Forum's topic. Depending on the topic there may be anything from just a handful of members to several thousand. A Forum on garden fence manufacture isn't going to get many interested members joining. One on computing will.

Libraries

Forum libraries are just like public libraries. They generally hold files associated with the topic of the Forum, although there's often an arguable overlap with other Forum library files. Forum members can contribute files to the libraries, or retrieve the files, as suits. Retrieving a file doesn't remove it from the library, it merely copies it to your computer, so it's still there for other members.

Getting around a Forum

My seven-year old asked me the other day when I was accessing a Forum "Where are they, daddy?" I enquired what on earth she was on about (I'm not the most patient of parents), to which she replied (she's not the most patient of children, neither) "Why, the four rooms, of course, silly!"

In many respects a Forum *is* like a collection of rooms. Each room holds different but related information, while the rooms themselves are linked by the corridor that is the **Forum Centre**. The rooms (well, OK let's get formal — *areas*) in a Forum depend largely on what the Forum is, and how it is organised, but they all have some areas in common — the Message Boards, the File Libraries, and the Forum Conferences — although what's in these areas can vary greatly.

Basic steps:

1 While they are not too difficult to get to grips with, new Forum users can easily get help and important information on entering a Forum, by clicking the **Getting Started** button

2 Read the Getting Started information (it is presented as a standard help file)

3 Close the window when you've got the information you need

A typical Forum

Click to change your identity

Click for information

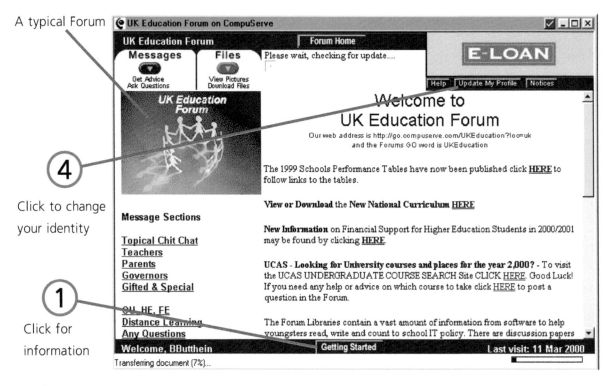

4 Initially, your User Name is used to identify you in a Forum, however you can change this to a another name if you want. Click the **Update My Profile** button to do this

5 Enter the name you want to be known by

6 Enter some of your interests, if you want

7 Click the **Update Profile** button

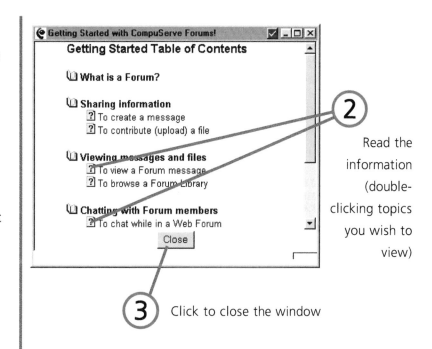

Read the information (double-clicking topics you wish to view)

Click to close the window

Enter your chosen name

Type in some interests (optional)

Click to enter the information

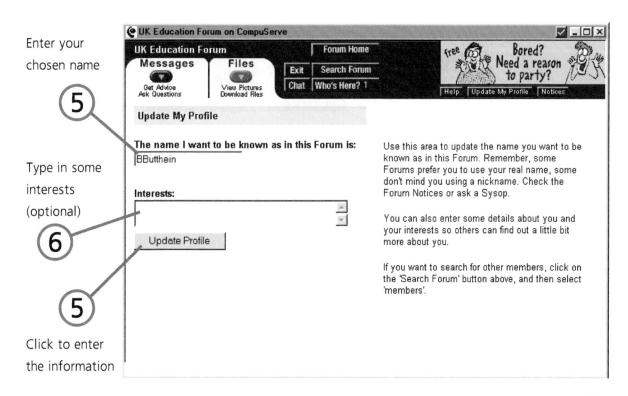

Message boards

Members of a Forum communicate with other members of the Forum in one of two ways. The first of these is through message boards.

Message boards are areas where a user posts a message, then other users post messages in reply. These collections of messages form conversations — *topics*.

Topics are grouped into sections (depending on their subject matter), and there can be many sections within a Forum message board (depending on the Forum).

Basic steps:

1 In a Forum, click the **Messages** tab

2 View the message sections in the Forum's message board — scroll down the list if necessary to locate the section you want — and click the message board section you want to open — it is hyperlinked

3 View the section topics— scroll down the list if necessary to locate the topic you want — click to open it

(1) Click a Forum's **Messages** tab

Locate the section you want to view and click it

(2)

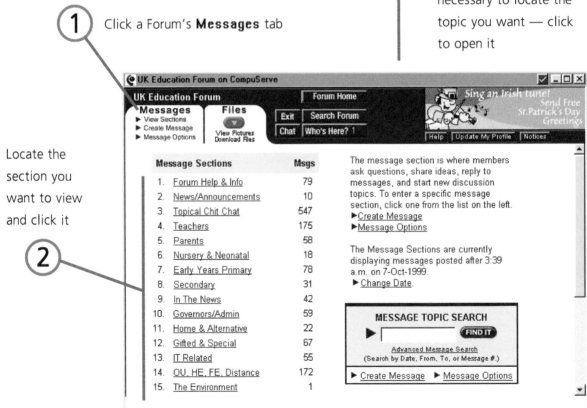

4 Click the message in that topic you want to read — the parent message opens by default

3 Locate the topic you want and click it

Take note:

Unlike mail messages (which are private communications) message boards allow members (and *only* members) to communicate in a public way. Other Forum members can read messages and indeed write their own messages for similar public display

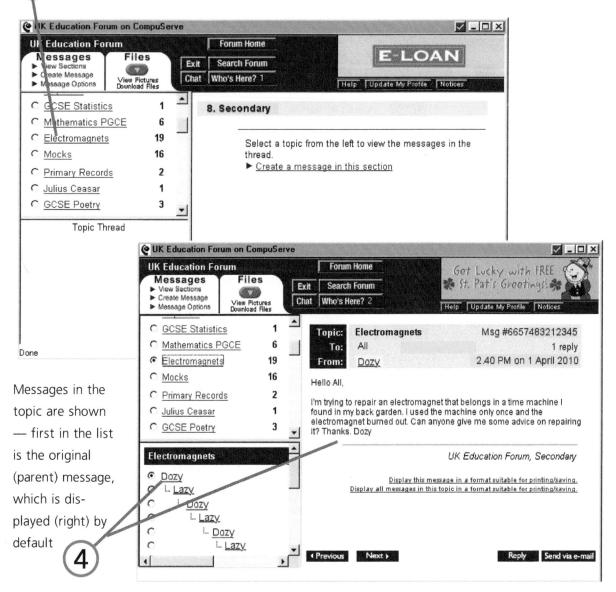

Messages in the topic are shown — first in the list is the original (parent) message, which is displayed (right) by default

4

Replying to a message

Basic steps:

Replying to a message in a topic is just like replying to a mail message you receive. The only difference is that — by default — not only can your recipient see your reply, but everyone else in the Forum can see it too if they wish.

1 Click the **Reply** button in the message window you wish to reply to

2 Type in the reply you want to give

3 Click **Send**

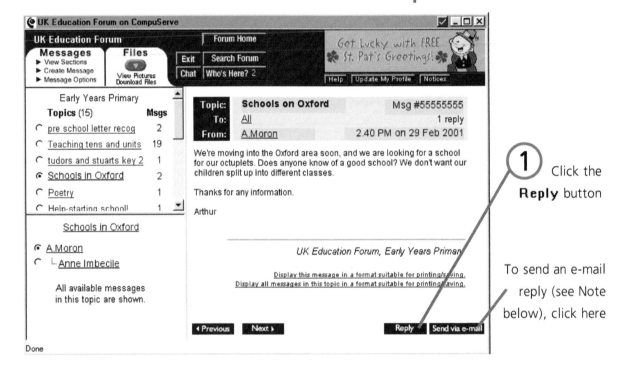

① Click the **Reply** button

To send an e-mail reply (see Note below), click here

Take note:

Remember that Forum message boards are public areas within CompuServe — in general, not only the person you're replying to will see your reply, but any other interested CompuServe member. In other words, Forum messages posted this way aren't private, so it's best to restrict your comments to non-personal ones. If you want to send a message directly to the person and not to have it posted on the message board you can do this in two ways: click the Send via e-mail button above, or follow the Tip right

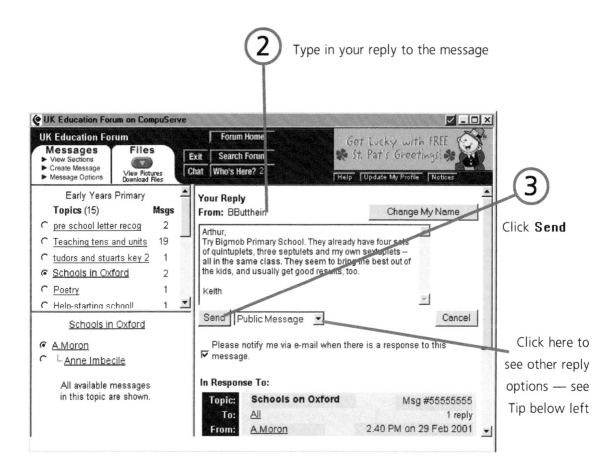

2 Type in your reply to the message

3 Click **Send**

Click here to see other reply options — see Tip below left

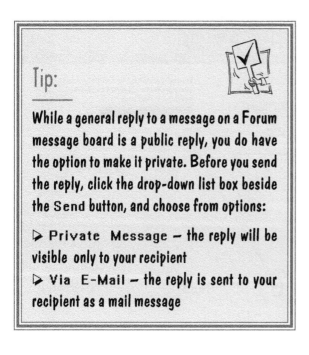

Tip:

While a general reply to a message on a Forum message board is a public reply, you do have the option to make it private. Before you send the reply, click the drop-down list box beside the Send button, and choose from options:

▷ Private Message – the reply will be visible only to your recipient
▷ Via E-Mail – the reply is sent to your recipient as a mail message

Tip:

Just as in conventional mail, CompuServe 2000 allows you to reply-quote in your reply (see pages 100–101 for full details of reply-quoting).

Just select the text you want to reply to, then hit the Reply button. The text is placed in the Your Reply window, preceded and suffixed with the reply-quoted characters (the symbols › and ‹, by default)

Creating a message topic

If no topics match the conversation you want to have, you can create your own. The easiest way to do this — and you can do it from anywhere in the messages section within a Forum — is to click a **Messages** tab sub-choice.

You don't have to be in any particular message section page for this — as you create a new message you have the option to choose which section you want to add the message to.

Basic steps:

1 Click the **Messages** tab of any **Forum**

2 In the Messages page, click the **Create Message** sub-choice of the **Messages** tab

3 Enter a subject

4 Write your message

5 Click the section drop-down list box and select a message section to create your message topic

6 Click the **Send** button

Get back to message sections page by clicking this **Message** tab sub-choice

Click the Messages tab

Click the **Create Message** sub-choice

Type your message subject here

Type the message here

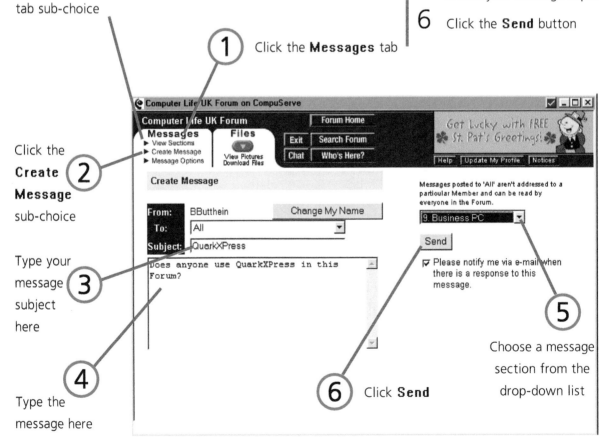

Choose a message section from the drop-down list

Click **Send**

contd...

Basic steps:

1 Click the **Files** tab of a Forum — the **File Sections** are displayed

2 Select the section you want

File retrieval

Files stored in Forum libraries are related to the main topic of the Forum. In other words, if you're looking for a particular type of file, go to the Forum where that topic is covered.

1 Click the **Files** tab

Select a section by clicking it

Tip:

If you know the name of a file you want – even if you only know part of its name – use the FILE KEYWORD SEARCH tool. Just enter the name or part-name, then click the FIND IT button – if the file's on CompuServe you'll be taken straight to it

File retrieval (contd)

Once you locate a file you want, it's an easy job to retrieve it from the Forum's file library to your computer. Note that the file can be any computer file — a word processed document, a computer game, a graphic image, a sound, a complete program. If it can be created and stored on a computer, and it's in the Forum's file libraries, you can download it.

Basic steps (contd):

3 In the file section locate the file you want and click it

4 Right-click the **Save File** hyperlink (that is, click it with the right mouse button)

5 Choose **Save Target As** from the drop-down menu

You can get back to the **File Sections** page by clicking here

Select the file you want to retrieve by clicking it

(3)

Choose **Save Target As** from the drop-down menu

(5)

(4) Right-click the Save File hyperlink

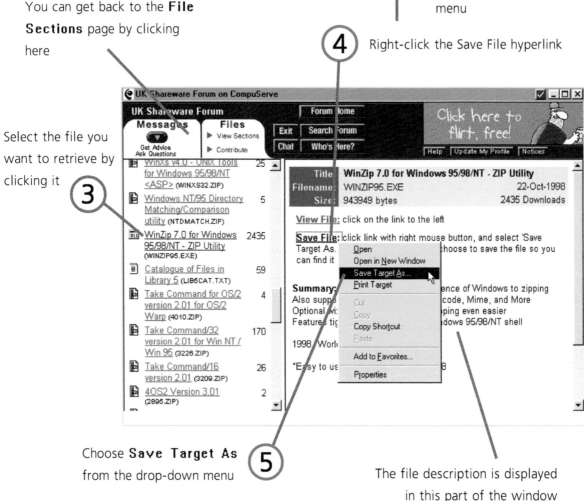

The file description is displayed in this part of the window

6 In the **Save As** dialog box, find a suitable location on your computer's hard drive to save the file

7 Click the **Save** button

8 The **File Download** dialog box shows the progress of the file download

After you complete step 5, the window right is briefly displayed as CompuServe 2000 locates the file and readies it for you to download — it is replaced rapidly by the **Save As** dialog box below

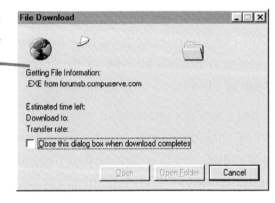

Use the various buttons in the Save As dialog box to locate somewhere to save the file — here, the CompuServe Downloads folder is used (but see the Tip below for a better place)

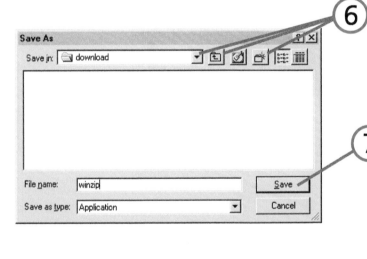

⑦ Click Save

The progress bar shows the file's download

⑧

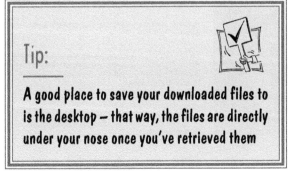

Tip:

A good place to save your downloaded files to is the desktop — that way, the files are directly under your nose once you've retrieved them

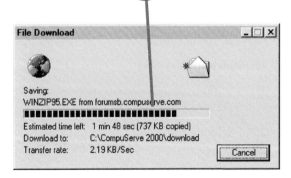

125

Contributing a file

Basic steps:

In a similar way to retrieving a file from a Forum library, you can contribute files to a library, too. Whereas file retrieval is also known as downloading, file contribution is also known as *uploading*.

There are no particular rules to file contribution, except that members are expected to upload only suitable files. Any files deemed not suitable by CompuServe will be removed, and members trying to do this repeatedly may be asked to leave.

1   In the Forum you want to contribute a file to, click the **Files** tab (if you haven't already done so)

2   Click the **Contribute** option of the Files tab

3   Click the drop-down menu list box and select a file section to contribute the file to

4   Click the **Contribute File** button

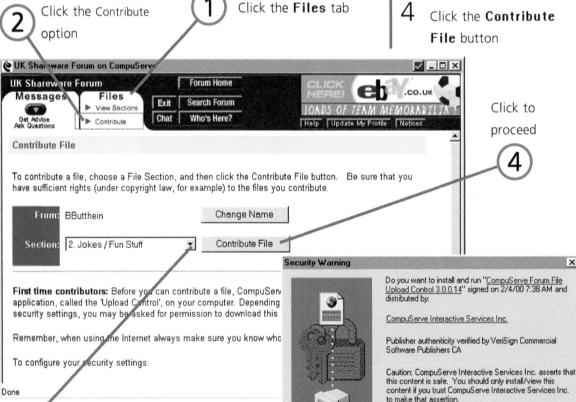

(2) Click the Contribute option

(1) Click the **Files** tab

(4) Click to proceed

(3) Select a file section

Click **Yes** (5)

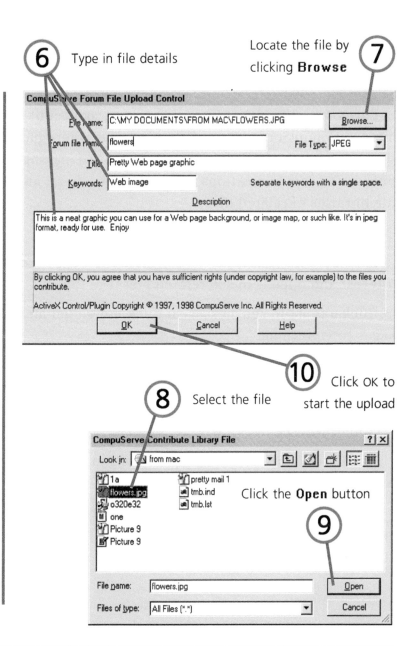

6 Type in file details

7 Locate the file by clicking **Browse**

CompuServe Forum File Upload Control

File name: C:\MY DOCUMENTS\FROM MAC\FLOWERS.JPG   Browse...

Forum file name: flowers   File Type: JPEG

Title: Pretty Web page graphic

Keywords: Web image   Separate keywords with a single space.

Description

This is a neat graphic you can use for a Web page background, or image map, or such like. It's in jpeg format, ready for use. Enjoy

By clicking OK, you agree that you have sufficient rights (under copyright law, for example) to the files you contribute.

ActiveX Control/Plugin Copyright © 1997, 1998 CompuServe Inc. All Rights Reserved.

OK   Cancel   Help

5 You will next see a security warning, offering you the option to install upload control software — click **Yes**

6 In the **Compuserve Forum File Upload Control** dialog box, enter details about the file you're contributing

7 Click the **Browse** button

8 In the **CompuServe Contribute Library File** dialog box, locate the file you want to contribute

9 Click the **Open** button

10 Back in the **Compuserve Forum File Upload Control** dialog box, click the **OK** button

8 Select the file

10 Click OK to start the upload

CompuServe Contribute Library File

Look in: from mac

1a
flowers.jpg
o320e32
one
Picture 9
Picture 9

pretty mail 1
tmb.ind
tmb.lst

Click the **Open** button

9

File name: flowers.jpg   Open

Files of type: All Files (*.*)   Cancel

Take note:

All files contributed by members of CompuServe are checked and vetted by Forum sysops prior to making them available for other members of the Forum. This is first to ensure they are suitable for general distribution, then to make sure they are virus free. So don't be surprised if your file isn't visible in the file library for some small time after you contribute it

Summary for Section 5

Forums are the places to go if you want to meet like-minded CompuServe users. They are areas where particular interests can be monitored. There are message boards for communications with other members, and file libraries of related files.

If you know the Forum name, **GO** to it.

In a Forum's **Messages** area, locate a section of interest and open it to see related message topics.

Click a topic to see messages. Click individual messages to view them.

Reply to messages either within the message area (your reply is made public — so anyone else using the Forum can see it), or reply by e-mail (so only the recipient will see it).

In a Forum's **Files** area, locate a section of interest and open it to see related files.

Retrieve files (download) from and contribute files (upload) to file libraries.

6 Technobobs

New User Names

A User Name is your online name. It's the name by which other CompuServe members know you. You choose your User Name, and others use it to identify you online. It can be simply your birthname, or a name you select to inform people something about you and your interests. It's the name you'll use in chat rooms, to send and receive Instant Messages, and mail.

When you first set up your account on the CompuServe network, you create a User Name (this is the Master User Name). While the Master User Name can't be changed (or deleted), you can create six other User Names (giving a total of seven) that *can* be changed or deleted as you want. You can allocate User Names to your family or friends, or even the staff of a small office. Each User Name has its own mail facilities and, of course, its own Personal Filing Cabinet.

Basic steps:

1 Choose **Access⤷User Names**, or **GO Names**

2 In the **Managing Member Names** dialog box, double-click **Create a User name**

3 In the resultant **Create a Member Name** dialog box, click the **Create** button

4 Enter the User Name you want to have

5 Click the **Create** button

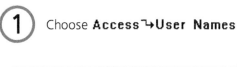

① Choose **Access⤷User Names**

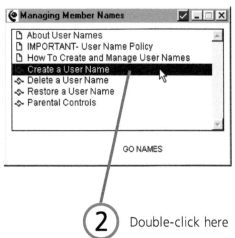

GO NAMES

② Double-click here

Take note:

As the Master User, you are incremental in setting up a User Name and assigning its password – effectively you are the *Controller of the CompuServe 2000 keys.*

Only you the Master User can delete User Names, or change their passwords

Tip:

Unless you're very lucky, you'll find that it's not so easy to create a User Name that's not already in use. After step 4, you may be presented with another dialog box that tells you the name is already used — there are over two million other CompuServe members, remember. Just keep trying until you pick a brand new User Name!

There's no hard-and-fast rule in finding a new User Name, except that putting numbers within the name somewhere can often be a good idea

Click the **Create** button ③

Create a Member Name _ □ ✕

Remember, you are known online by your User Name, which is also the first part of your e-mail address (i.e., UserName@cs.com), so give careful consideration to the one you choose. Your User Name is unique to you; if someone else has already taken the name you request, you'll be asked to select another one.

Please be sure to read the User Name Policy, available from the previous menu, for rules regarding appropriate User Names.

Create   Cancel

Take note:

CompuServe encourages users to be creative when setting up new User Names — but requests that users be responsible. In other words — please don't create rude names which might offend.

CompuServe reserves the right to delete offensive names, or request that they be deleted by the user

⑤ Click **Create**

Read the description, then enter the new User Name you want here

Create a Member Name

Each account may have up to seven Member Names at one time. A Member Name may be from 3 to 16 characters (letters, numbers, and/or spaces). The first character in the Member Name must be a letter, and will be capitalized automatically. The rest of the characters will appear just as you enter them.

E.g. "Ski Racer", "JohnDoe123"

④

Please type the Member Name you want to use:

csmail4me

Create   Cancel

New User Names (contd)

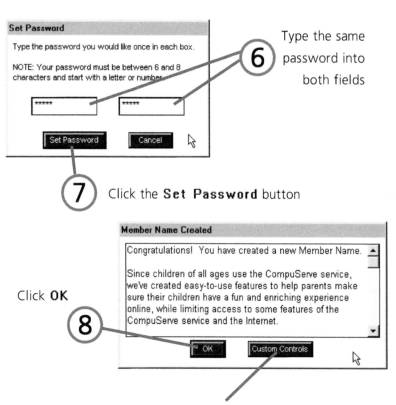

Type the same password into both fields

Click the **Set Password** button

Click **OK**

The **Custom Controls** button lets you set features allocated to User Names — if a child has a User Name, say, you might wish to restrict which Internet sites can be accessed when that User Name is logged on — see pages 138–139

6 If your desired User Name is acceptable (that is, it's not already is use by someone else), the **Set Password** dialog box will be displayed. Enter your chosen password into both fields

7 Click the **Set Password** button

8 If your password is acceptable, the **Member Name Created** dialog box is displayed. Click the **OK** button to close it

9 Back in the **Managing Member Names** dialog box, click the close box

Click to close

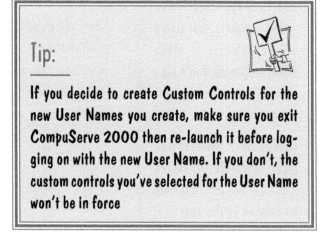

Tip:

If you decide to create Custom Controls for the new User Names you create, make sure you exit CompuServe 2000 then re-launch it before logging on with the new User Name. If you don't, the custom controls you've selected for the User Name won't be in force

Basic steps:

1 Launch CompuServe 2000

2 Click the drop-down menu arrow of the **Select User Name** field in the **Connect to CompuServe** dialog box

3 Click the User Name you want to log onto CompuServe using

4 Click the **Connect** button

New User Name logon

When you want to connect to CompuServe with one of your new User Names, you have two options:

▷ you can choose the User Name before you connect — this is probably the best for general use — see below

▷ you can switch User Names while you are connected to CompuServe — see over the page.

With either method you need to be aware that each User Name has a password. A user logging on with any particular User Name therefore needs to know and use that password.

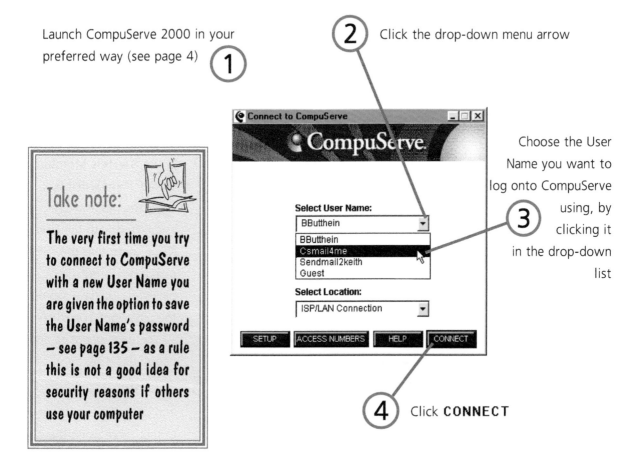

Launch CompuServe 2000 in your preferred way (see page 4) **1**

2 Click the drop-down menu arrow

Take note:

The very first time you try to connect to CompuServe with a new User Name you are given the option to save the User Name's password — see page 135 — as a rule this is not a good idea for security reasons if others use your computer

Choose the User Name you want to log onto CompuServe using, by clicking it in the drop-down list **3**

Connect to CompuServe

CompuServe

Select User Name:

BButthein

BButthein
Csmail4me
Sendmail2keith
Guest

Select Location:

ISP/LAN Connection

SETUP   ACCESS NUMBERS   HELP   CONNECT

4 Click **CONNECT**

Switching User Names

You can also log on to CompuServe with a different User Name while connected to CompuServe. This is called *switching User Names*. While this means you can log on with a different User Name while you're online, so is undoubtedly useful (you don't need to make a new telephone call each time you want to switch, for example), it is still subject to the same password conditions noted on the previous page.

Choose **Access**↪**Switch User Names** ①

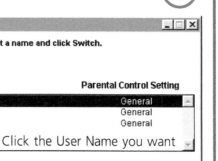

Enter the ⑤ password

Click to connect using the selected ⑥ User Name

1 While connected to CompuServe, choose **Access**↪**Switch User Name**

2 In the **Switch User Names** dialog box, click the User Name you wish to switch to

3 Click **Switch** (or simply double-click the User Name you want at step 2)

4 The **Switch User Name** dialog box gives you information about online time and billing for the previous User Name. Click **Continue** to proceed

5 In the **Switch Member Name Password** box, enter the password associated with the User Name (note that this dialog box is not displayed if you have stored the password previously — see page opposite and pages 136–137

6 Click **OK**, whereupon you will be connected to CompuServe using the selected User Name

New name password

1 Enter the password you previously used at step 6 on page 132, in the **Password** field — it will be displayed as asterisks

2 Type the same password in the **Confirm Password** field

3 Click **OK**

NOT SAVING A PASSWORD:

4 Click **Cancel**

Take note:

If you save a password associated with any User Name, then any other user who uses your computer will be able to log onto CompuServe using your User Name – so will be able to read your mail, chat to others, and do everything that you usually do.

For security reasons, therefore, it's not a good idea to store a password

If this is the first time you have attempted to connect to CompuServe using any particular User Name you will be offered the opportunity of storing the password associated with the name on your computer. After you have followed step 3 on page 133, you have two options which to need to consider carefully:

▷ you can store the password — thereafter, when logging on as shown on page 133 you won't need to enter a password, and steps 1–4 there are all you need

▷ you can opt *not* to store a password — so you will need to enter the password each time you attempt to log on. This is the most secure option.

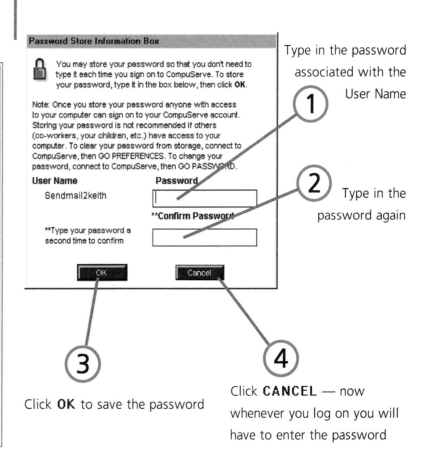

Type in the password associated with the User Name

① Type in the password again

② Type in the password again

③ Click **OK** to save the password

④ Click **CANCEL** — now whenever you log on you will have to enter the password

Password control

At any time, you can change the password associated with any User Name. You do this in two ways:

▷ you can change the password to a new one

▷ you can change whether your password is stored on your computer or not.

For either procedure, you need to be connected to CompuServe. As a general note — for security reasons — it's always best not to store your password on your computer.

CHANGING YOUR PASSWORD:

1 While logged on, choose **Access▸Passwords**, or **GO Password**

2 In the resultant **Change Your Password** dialog box, click **Change**

3 In the next dialog box, enter the old password, enter the new password, and confirm your new password in the appropriate fields

4 Click the **Change** button

5 Click **OK** in the next dialog box

(2) Click **Change**

Change Your Password

Your password should be easy for you to remember, but not for others to guess. Do NOT use your first name, your User Name, or other obvious words as your password. Your password must be 6 to 8 characters long.
You should change your password frequently. Never give it to anyone. Compuserve employees will never ask for your password.
NOTE: Anyone who knows (or can guess) your password has full access to your account.

[Change]   [Cancel]

Go: PASSWORD

Enter the old password, then your
new one and confirm it

(3)

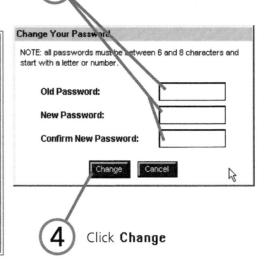

Change Your Password

NOTE: all passwords must be between 6 and 8 characters and start with a letter or number.

Old Password: [   ]

New Password: [   ]

Confirm New Password: [   ]

[Change] [Cancel]

(4) Click **Change**

Take note:

Steps 1–4 allow you to change the password associated only with the User Name you have logged on with. Similarly, steps 5–10 only allow you to adjust the password locally for the User Name that's logged on. To change another User Name's password you need to log on with the other User Name first

6 While logged on, choose **Access⤷Preferences**

7 In the resultant window, click the **Passwords** icon

8 Enter the password in the **Store Passwords** dialog box

9 Click controls appropriately

10 Click **OK**

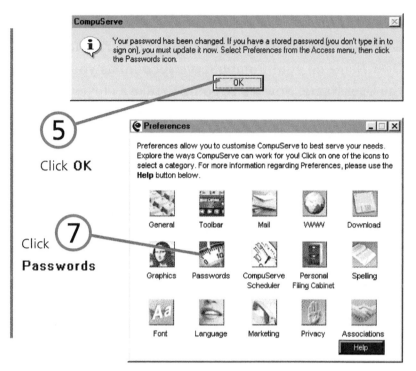

Click **OK**

Click ⑦
Passwords

Type in your new password

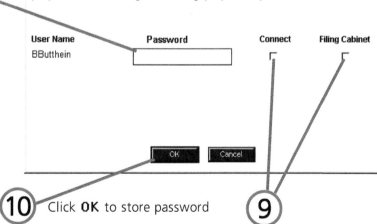

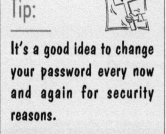

Tip:

It's a good idea to change your password every now and again for security reasons.

Also, use passwords that aren't obvious to others. Don't use your spouse's name, for example

Click **OK** to store password

Check the **Connect** box to allow you to connect without having to enter your password. Uncheck the **Filing Cabinet** checkbox to be able to open your Personal Filing Cabinet without having to enter your password

Parental Controls

On page 132 we saw how you can set controls for each User Name on your CompuServe account as you create the User Name. Now we're going to take a closer look at the process — called Parental Controls — and see how to set the controls at any time.

Members (parents, in this case) have one account, which can have up to seven User Names on it at any time. The first User Name (the one you got when you first used CompuServe 2000) is the *master account*. Any other User Names (for the kids, say) are known as *sub-accounts*.

Here we look at how to set parental controls for a sub-account's e-mail feature. Parental controls for other features are similar.

Basic steps:

1 Connect to CompuServe, using the master account User Name

2 **GO Parental controls**

3 Click the **Set Parental Controls now** radio button

4 Choose the User Name you wish to set controls for, from the drop-down menu

5 Click the arrow icon alongside the type of controls you wish to set — here we set them for e-mail

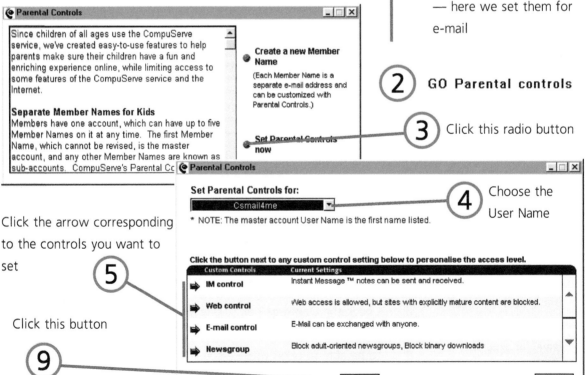

① Logon to CompuServe

② **GO Parental controls**

③ Click this radio button

④ Choose the User Name

Click the arrow corresponding to the controls you want to set ⑤

Click this button ⑨

138

6 In the **Mail Controls** dialog box for that user, set the controls to suit

7 Click the **OK** button

8 In the confirmation dialog box, click the **OK** button

9 Back in the **Parental Controls** dialog box, click **Done**

Allow or block e-mail from all or some places

Block only attachments and graphics

If you block email from some addresses and domains, you need to tell CompuServe which addresses or domains are blocked. Type them in the entry field first, then click **Add** to list them below

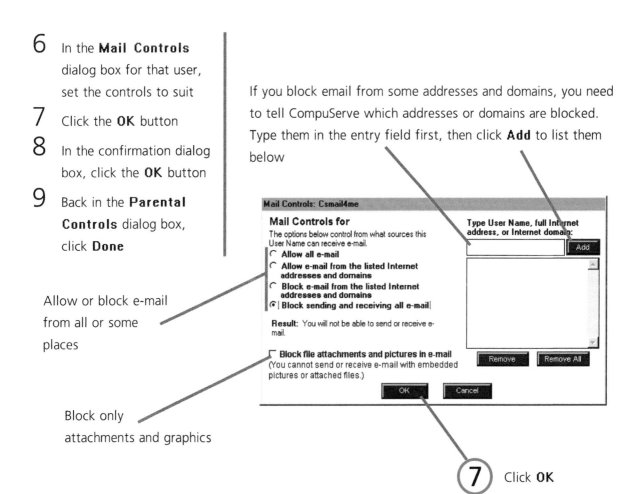

7 Click **OK**

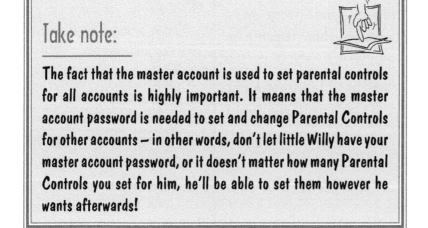

Take note:

The fact that the master account is used to set parental controls for all accounts is highly important. It means that the master account password is needed to set and change Parental Controls for other accounts – in other words, don't let little Willy have your master account password, or it doesn't matter how many Parental Controls you set for him, he'll be able to set them however he wants afterwards!

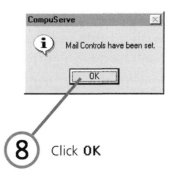

8 Click **OK**

139

Attachment strategy

You shouldn't assume that the people you send files to — your recipients — will be able to use attached files directly.

You must make sure the file itself is in a format your recipient can handle once it's arrived at its destination. There are several reasons why file attachment might be a problem, including:

▷ people use different computer platforms eg, Windows 3.1, Windows 95, Windows 98, Windows NT, Windows 2000, Unix, Linux, MacOS. Programs for one platform don't usually run on another platform

▷ people use different programs — does your recipient have the same word processor, spreadsheet, database, graphics program as you?

▷ different versions of the same programs may have different file types — typically, an older version of the same program won't be able to open a file saved from a newer program version

▷ some e-mail programs (CompuServe 2000 included) automatically compress files prior to sending as attachments. If a recipient doesn't have the means to decompress a file — say a different email program is used to receive the mail message — then the file is unreadable.

With all this in mind, it's obvious that file attachment can't be taken lightly. However, the strategy here should help to reduce problems.

Ask your recipient if the file you are going to attach will be usable:

1 If it's an application, will the recipient's computer be able to run it? Does the recipient have the same type of computer, the same operating system, enough memory, and so on?

2 If it's a document, does the recipient have the same application that created the document?

3 Will the recipient's equivalent application open the document? Does it convert documents from other formats to the application's own format?

4 Can your recipient's e-mail program cope with file attachments (CompuServe 2000, along with most recently developed e-mail programs, automatically does this, but some don't — does your recipient know what to do with attached files in this case)?

- mail between users is transmitted in a pure text format

- anything else (graphics files, word processor documents, applications, spreadsheets files, databases) is called binary

- text is common to all computers, of all makes, of all operating systems, of all types

- binary files are usually specific to particular computer applications — you might not be able to open one file with another computer application

- binary files are converted to pure text files by CompuServe 2000 before thay are sent attached to mail messages, then need to be converted back on receipt to binary format

- it's very common to compress binary files that have been converted to text prior to sending as attachments, to help keep online times (and hence phone bills) down

The lowest common denominator

After you've followed the steps on the left, you're in a position to decide how best to attach a file. The general rule is to stick to the 'lowest common denominator' between yourself and your recipient.

If you *know* your recipient has the same application the file was created in, you can send the file directly. If not, convert the file to a common format which the two applications can share. For example, save a word processed file in *rich text format* (RTF) to make sure that any modern word processor is able to open the file.

Forewarned is forearmed

Read pages 64–65 about file encoding and compression. Arm yourself with the tools suggested there to encode, decode, compress and decompress files of most formats so that you can:

a) convert files before you attach them to a format your recipient will be able to handle

and

b) convert files you receive to a format you can handle.

> **Tip:**
>
> The lowest common denominator of all when it comes to mail is text. Save a document as text before attaching it, then just about any computer, with any program, will be able to use it on receipt

141

Contact List

The CompuServe 2000 Contact List is a clever tool that tells you when your friends, family, or colleagues are online. After this you can send them, say, an Instant Message, or mail them, knowing they will get your message or mail immediately.

First though, you need to set up your Contact List, to contain the friends, family and colleagues you want.

(**1**) Connect to CompuServe

(**2**) Choose **People⤷Setup Contact List**

(**3**) Select a group

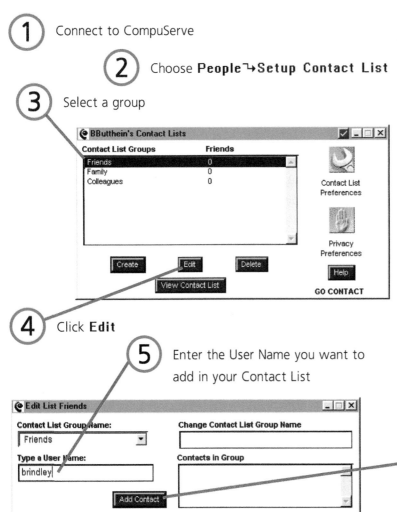

(**4**) Click **Edit**

(**5**) Enter the User Name you want to add in your Contact List

(**6**) Click the **Add Contact** button

Basic steps:

1 Connect to CompuServe

2 Choose **People⤷Setup Contact List**

3 Select a Contact List group, by clicking it

4 Click the **Edit** button, or double-click the group at step 3

5 In the **Edit List** for the Contact List group you selected, type a User Name

6 Click the **Add Contact** button

7 Note that the User Name you entered is placed in the **Contacts in Groups** field — repeat steps 5 & 6 to include further contacts

8 Click the **Save** button

9 In the confirmation dialog box, click the **OK** button

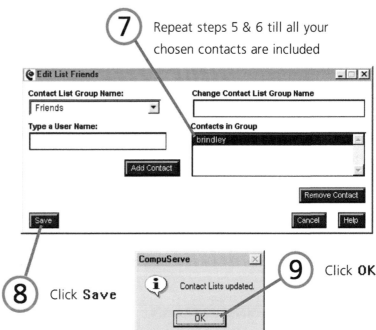

7 Repeat steps 5 & 6 till all your chosen contacts are included

10 Back in the **Contact Lists** dialog box, click the **View Contact List** button

11 The **Contact Lists Groups** window shows all your contacts, as groups. With this on-screen while online, you can see when contacts are also online

Edit List Friends

Contact List Group Name:
Friends

Change Contact List Group Name

Type a User Name:

Contacts in Group
brindley

Add Contact

Remove Contact

Save

Cancel   Help

8 Click **Save**

CompuServe

ⓘ Contact Lists updated.

OK

9 Click **OK**

Any groups you added contacts to now show the numbers of contacts added

BButthein's Contact Lists

Contact List Groups   Friends
Friends   1
Family   0
Colleagues   0

Contact List Preferences

Privacy Preferences

Create   Edit   Delete

View Contact List

Help

GO CONTACT

Tip:

The Contact Lists Groups window and the Contact Lists dialog box are vital components of your Contact List. Get from one to the other by clicking the View Contact List button of the Contact Lists dialog box, and by clicking the Setup button of the Contact Lists Groups window

10 Click **View Contact List**

11

Contact List Groups
Contacts Online
Friends (0/1)
Family (0/0)
Colleagues (0/0)

Instant Message™   Setup

GO: CONTACT VIEW

Keep the **Contact Lists Groups** window on-screen all the time you are online — this way you can see instantly if any of your chosen contacts are online

143

Contact List (contd)

You can fine-tune the Contact List and how it works by adjusting its preferences. First you can specify how your Contact List works for you. Then you can also specify how *your* User Name is used by other people's Contact Lists.

YOUR CONTACT LIST:

1 Connect to CompuServe

2 Choose **People↪Setup Contact List**

3 Click the **Contact List Preferences** button

4 Select the options you want, by checking (or unchecking) the various controls' checkboxes

5 Click **Save**

6 In the confirmation dialog box, click **OK**

(1) Connect to CompuServe

(2) Choose **People↪Setup Contact List**

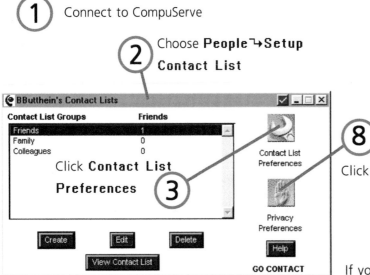

Click **Contact List Preferences** **(3)**

(8) Click

If you choose to play sounds at step 4, get them from the CompuServe Sound Library

Choose the controls you want for your Contact List: **(4)**

check to display the Contact Lists Groups window as you go online

check to play a sound as a contact comes online

check to play a sound as a contact goes offline

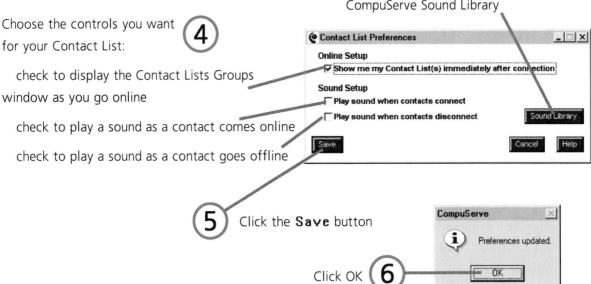

(5) Click the **Save** button

Click OK **(6)**

⑦ Follow steps 1 & 2

Click **Add** ⑩

⑨ Enter a User Name

OTHERS' CONTACT LISTS:

7 Follow steps 1 & 2

8 Click the **Privacy Preferences** button

9 In the **Privacy Preferences** dialog box, type in the User Name you want to set options for

10 Click the **Add** button

11 Repeat steps 9 & 10 to add further User Names

12 Select the controls you wish to adjust

13 Click **Save**

14 In the confirmation dialog box, click **OK**

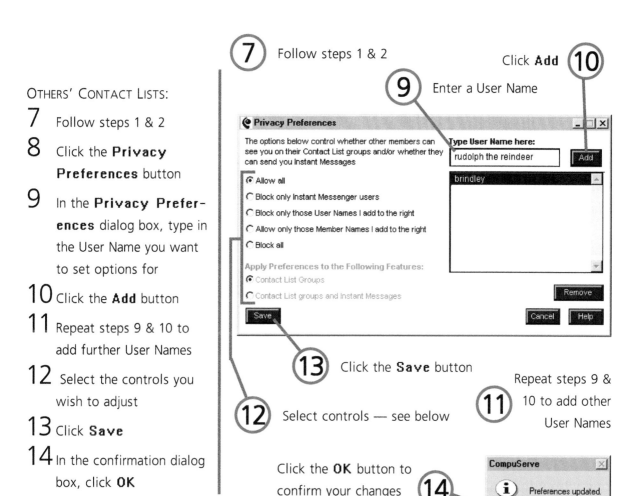

⑬ Click the **Save** button

⑫ Select controls — see below

⑪ Repeat steps 9 & 10 to add other User Names

Click the **OK** button to confirm your changes ⑭

Privacy Preferences controls

The controls in the Privacy Preferences dialog box allow you to specify whether other users can or cannot contact you, in various ways — the most important are:

▷ **Allow all** — you don't need to add any users — they can all contact you (this is the default)

▷ **Block only those User Names I add to the Right** — allows you to specify who *cannot* contact you

▷ **Allow only those User names I add to the right** — allows you to specify who *can* contact you.

Tip:

Occasionally, you might get a persistent user sending you Instant Messages frequently. Use the Privacy Preferences to make sure they can't pester you

145

Autonotification

Basic steps:

1 Connect to CompuServe

2 **GO Autonotify**

3 Check the **Enable E-Mail Address Notification** checkbox

4 Click the **OK** button

If you've started to use CompuServe 2000 having already had an earlier CompuServe account, your earlier account's mail details will be held on record by CompuServe. Any mail sent to you addressed to your earlier account in any of the previous forms (known as *classic* mail):

▷ 1030405987,10239

▷ 1030405987.10239@compuserve.com

▷ username

▷ username@compuserve.com

▷ username@csi.com

will be automatically forwarded to you, freely and indefinitely, to your CompuServe 2000 mailbox. So there's no need to worry about losing any mail. However, If you *do* have an earlier account (in other words — this doesn't concern users who have only ever used CompuServe 2000) then it's a good idea to inform anyone who might mail you of your new mail address.

To do this, you can setup a process within CompuServe to send anyone who sends you a mail message an automatic reply that tells them your new mail address. The process is called *autonotification*.

Take note:

While the Autonotification process is automatic once you've set it up, it's rather impersonal — just imagine your Mum receiving an automatic reply telling her that you've changed your address — so it's always the best idea to personally tell everyone who you expect to mail you that you've changed address. After all, it's good to... err, talk

(1) Log on to CompuServe

(2) **GO Autonotify**

Check this checkbox

(3)

(4) Click **OK**

E-Mail Address Notification

We recommend you contact all your e-mail correspondents personally to inform them of your new e-mail address.

Your e-mail will be automatically forwarded from your old address to your new address. You can click **Enable E-Mail Address Notification** to send a message confirming your new address to anyone who uses your old address.

☐ **Enable E-Mail Address Notification**

[OK] [Cancel]

Basic steps:

1 Connect to CompuServe
2 **GO Billing**
3 In the **Membership Options** dialog box, click the **Your Bill** hyperlink
4 In the **Manage Your Account** dialog box, click the **Current Bill Summary** hyperlink
5 View your account details

Billing

OK, so you're online and having fun. You're surfing the Internet and mailing all your friends, family and colleagues. You're like a human vacuum cleaner — scouring the Web and downloading all the goodies you can get your sticky modem on. But nothing this good can be free. So, how much is all this fun costing you?

Fortunately, it's easy to find out.

(1) Connect to CompuServe

(2) **GO Billing**

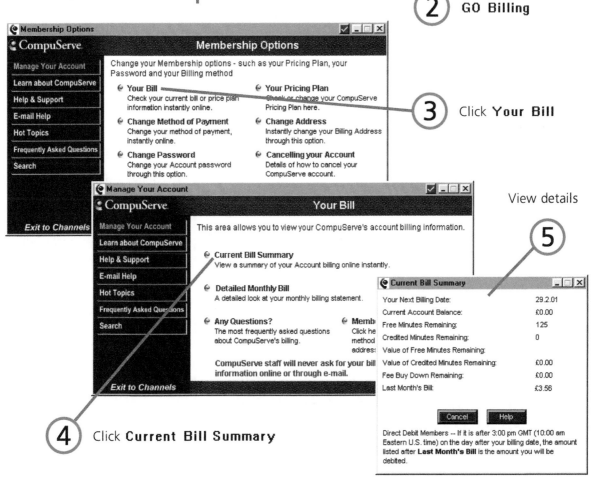

(3) Click **Your Bill**

View details

(4) Click **Current Bill Summary**

147

Connecting while abroad

Unlike the vast majority of Internet service providers, CompuServe is a worldwide network. This has many advantages, not the least being that you can connect to CompuServe (to access your mail, surf the Internet, and so on) wherever you might be in the world.

All you need do is make sure the correct telephone number for your location is set within CompuServe 2000 on your computer before you go on a trip.

(1) Connect to CompuServe

(2) Choose **Access↪ CompuServe Access Numbers**

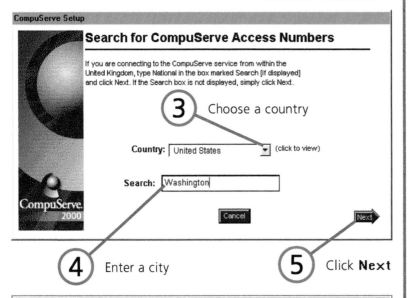

CompuServe Setup

Search for CompuServe Access Numbers

If you are connecting to the CompuServe service from within the United Kingdom, type National in the box marked Search [if displayed] and click Next. If the Search box is not displayed, simply click Next.

(3) Choose a country

Country: [United States ▾] (click to view)

Search: [Washington]

[Cancel] [Next]

(4) Enter a city

(5) Click **Next**

Take note:

Once you've completed the steps here, your new location (along with its telephone numbers) is stored, and accessible in the CompuServe 2000 Connect Screen — just choose it from the Select Location drop-down menu when you are at that location

Basic steps:

1 Connect to CompuServe

2 Choose **Access↪ CompuServe Access Numbers**

3 In the **CompuServe Setup** dialog box, click the **Country** drop-down menu and choose the country you will be visiting

4 Type in the city you will be visiting

5 Click the **Next** button

6 Choose **Add Location**, from the **Add Numbers to this Location** drop-down menu

7 Enter a name for the location

8 Click **OK**

9 Select a number from the list

10 Click the **Add** button

11 Click **OK**

12 Repeat steps 9 and 10, for further numbers (CompuServe recommends at least two)

13 Click Next

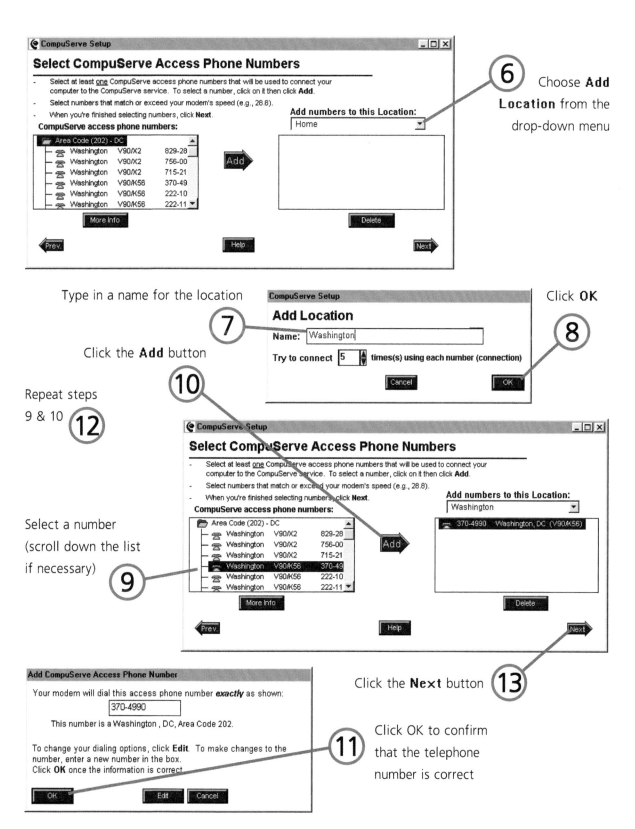

CompuServe Setup ▬ □ ✕

Select CompuServe Access Phone Numbers

- Select at least one CompuServe access phone numbers that will be used to connect your computer to the CompuServe service. To select a number, click on it then click **Add**.
- Select numbers that match or exceed your modem's speed (e.g., 28.8).
- When you're finished selecting numbers, click **Next**.

CompuServe access phone numbers:

Add numbers to this Location:
Home ▼

Area Code (202) - DC		
☎ Washington	V90/X2	829-28
☎ Washington	V90/X2	756-00
☎ Washington	V90/X2	715-21
☎ Washington	V90/K56	370-49
☎ Washington	V90/K56	222-10
☎ Washington	V90/K56	222-11 ▼

Add ▶

More Info   Delete

◀ Prev.   Help   Next ▶

⑥ Choose **Add Location** from the drop-down menu

Type in a name for the location

⑦

CompuServe Setup

Add Location

Name: Washington

Try to connect 5 ▲▼ **times(s) using each number (connection)**

Cancel   OK

Click **OK**

⑧

Click the **Add** button

⑩

Repeat steps 9 & 10 **⑫**

CompuServe Setup ▬ □ ✕

Select CompuServe Access Phone Numbers

- Select at least one CompuServe access phone numbers that will be used to connect your computer to the CompuServe service. To select a number, click on it then click **Add**.
- Select numbers that match or exceed your modem's speed (e.g., 28.8).
- When you're finished selecting numbers, click **Next**.

CompuServe access phone numbers:

Add numbers to this Location:
Washington ▼

Select a number (scroll down the list if necessary) **⑨**

Area Code (202) - DC		
☎ Washington	V90/X2	829-28
☎ Washington	V90/X2	756-00
☎ Washington	V90/X2	715-21
☎ Washington	V90/K56	370-49
☎ Washington	V90/K56	222-10
☎ Washington	V90/K56	222-11 ▼

Add ▶

☎ 370-4990	Washington, DC (V90/K56)

More Info   Delete

◀ Prev.   Help   Next ▶

Click the **Next** button **⑬**

Add CompuServe Access Phone Number

Your modem will dial this access phone number *exactly* as shown:

370-4990

This number is a Washington , DC, Area Code 202.

To change your dialing options, click **Edit**. To make changes to the number, enter a new number in the box.
Click **OK** once the information is correct.

OK   Edit   Cancel

⑪ Click OK to confirm that the telephone number is correct

149

Summary for Section 6

Add new User Names to your master account — each account can hold a total of seven User Names, including the master account name.

Logon with a User Name, or switch User Names while you're connected.

Set passwords for your User Names.

Set parental controls for each User Name — you can restrict a User Name's access to services considerably if you want to.

When you attach files to mail messages, make sure the file can be received and used correctly by your recipient.

Your Contact List is the place to keep details of the friends, family, and colleagues that you might want to send an Instant Message to.

GO Autonotify to instruct the CompuServe service to send a message informing anyone who tries to mail you that your address has changed.

GO Billing to find out your account's status.

Set locations before you move your computer, to make sure you can still connect to CompuServe while you're there.

Index

Printed and bound by CPI Group (UK) Ltd, Croydon, CR0 4YY

22/10/2024

01777635-0011